CASTLE SINCLAIR, WICK : J CAMPBELL KERR

WHERE'S THAT?

The approximate locations of our picture features

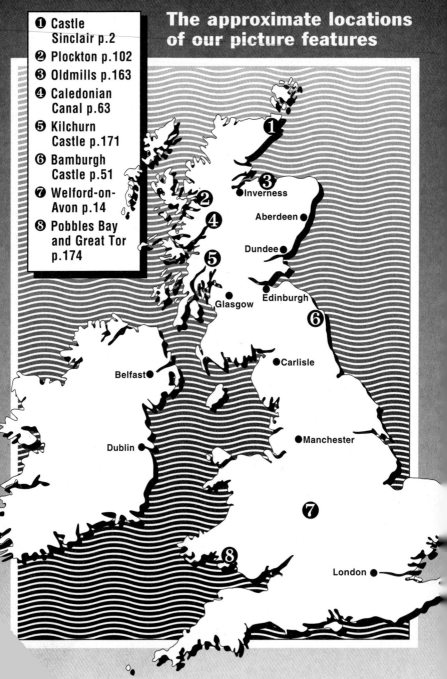

People's Friend Annual 1998

Contents

BACK COVER St Andrew's Parish Church, Dundee.

ARE you all right, Sharon?" Mrs McBain, the manageress of Gracious Living Home Caterers, looked sharply at her assistant. Sharon Bell came in for the last of the trays to load into the van that was waiting at the door of the shop.

"Yes. I'm fine, Mrs McBain," Sharon replied, with what she hoped was a convincing smile.

She knew that her boss had been doubtful about letting her take on Mr Kirkwood's birthday-lunch. Mainly because Mr Kirkwood was a new client, and a fairly well-off one, and the firm was hopeful of receiving more business from him in future.

"I just thought you were looking pale," Mrs McBain said anxiously.

"I expect it's that new make-up I tried this morning." Sharon smiled. "It's making me look pale and interesting."

"Oh, that's it, is it?" Mrs McBain laughed.

But when Sharon climbed into the back of the van behind Peter Gray, the driver, and Julie, the waitress, her smile faded. Every time she thought of the shock she had received that morning, when she opened the letter from the bank, she felt quite sick again.

How could James have done it to her? She relived the scene again as Peter drove them out of the town centre and into the pleasant western suburbs.

"An overdraft of five hundred pounds!" she had cried. "Look, James! They've made some daft mistake. You'll have to phone them up. Or I can call in today after work."

"No point in doing that," he had said quietly, not turning round from the cooker, where he had three slices of toast under the grill. "It's not a mistake, Sharon."

"What do you mean?" She had gasped. "Not a mistake! It must be. Surely we haven't spent all that money!"

"It's more easily done than you think," James had said. "That repair to my car ran away with two hundred. Then we bought that new washing-machine. And the freezer. And the microwave oven

OF LOVE

by Elsie Jackson

to make it easier for you when you came home from work."

"But James!" Sharon had protested. "I wouldn't have had any of those things, if I hadn't thought we could afford them. You kept saying we were all right! No wonder you shoved the bank statements away before I could see them! How long has this overdraft been growing?"

"A few months," James had said reluctantly, as he poured out her coffee.

"And you never said anything to me about it!"

"I thought I could pay it off," he had said miserably. "I didn't want to worry you."

"And I trusted you!" she had cried bitterly. "That's the worst part of it all. You lied to me. And I believed you."

"Don't you see?" he had pleaded with her. "I wanted you to have as much as all the other working wives we know. I know it was stupid. But I did it because I love you, Sharon."

"That's no excuse," she had said hotly. "We've only been married two years and you've deceived me like this."

"I'll go and see the bank manager," he had told her. "I'll make some arrangement about paying it off. And it will never happen again, Sharon. I promise."

"I can't forgive you!" she had cried as she ran out to catch the bus to her work.

"Mrs Bell!" Young Julie was looking over her shoulder and trying to attract Sharon's attention. "Peter wants to know what number in Acacia Avenue we're going to."

"Forty-two," said Sharon, forcing herself to smile. "It's a big place, apparently. Mr Kirkwood's a retired businessman and very well off."

"Did you say it was his eightieth birthday?" Julie asked.

"Yes. That's right. The old gentleman's wife died last year, and he's been rather depressed. So his nephews and nieces decided to get together and organise a birthday lunch for him."

"Oh! Wasn't that nice!" exclaimed young Julie, smiling.

"Yes," said Sharon. "And they've ordered the most expensive menu Mrs McBain could provide. Caviar and champagne, for a start."

"Gosh!" Peter chuckled. "I can bet no-one will treat me like that when I'm eighty. I'll be lucky if my relations lay on crisps and lemonade."

"Ah! But you don't live in a mansion like this, Peter," Julie breathed as they turned into the tree-lined gravelled drive. "He must have pots of money."

MONEY! I hate the very sound of the word, Sharon thought bitterly, as she went back and forth between Mr Kirkwood's kitchen and dining-room, replenishing the gaps in the magnificent cold buffet that she and Mrs McBain had prepared last night and this morning. She could not help occasionally casting envious glances round the party guests and thinking that none of them would have any money worries on their mind.

"Did you see those pearls?" young Julie would whisper to Sharon, eyes like saucers, as she popped into the luxuriously-appointed kitchen. Or, "That lady in the red dress has six diamonds in her ring!"

The conversation was all about skiing holidays, and escaping to the sun next winter, or "We're thinking of trying a cruise on the QE2."

And I would have been content with a day at Dunoon, Sharon thought bitterly. If only he had been honest with me. That's what hurts. That's what's ruined everything.

"Do you think the old gentleman's enjoyed himself, Mrs Bell?" Julie asked anxiously, when the party was in full swing. "He doesn't look very pleased."

Sharon came to with a start, flushing guiltily. She had been so engrossed in her own unhappy thoughts that she had been neglecting her duties. The first rule of Gracious Living Home Caterers was to make sure that the client was satisfied. And up until now she had hardly looked at poor old Mr Kirkwood.

S HE looked anxiously across the room now, to where he was sitting in the big easy-chair by the fireside, surveying his guests. He must have been a big, powerful man in his young days, she thought. Even now he looked strong.

He was wearing a sweater, having refused to change into a suit. She had heard his guests remarking on this with some amusement! His white hair was still plentiful, and he had bushy eyebrows, from beneath which a pair of sharp, blue eyes took in all that was going on.

But Julie was right. There was a decidedly disgruntled look about him. She wondered if any of the food had not been up to standard. She doubted it, for she and Mrs McBain had taken great pains with it. More likely it was the wine. Sharon was not a great expert on wines, though she had a basic knowledge that had enabled her to get through her catering course.

I ought to have asked him before this, she thought vexedly. But better late than never.

She walked over to Mr Kirkwood's side, then in the discreet way in which she had been trained, she leaned over and spoke softly.

"I hope everything was to your satisfaction, Mr Kirkwood?"

She half-hoped the old gentleman would say, like ninety-nine per cent. of Gracious Living's clients, "Yes. Fine. Just fine."

He did not, though. He turned and looked at her for a long time with his penetrating blue eyes, then replied quietly. "I wonder if you would have the goodness to stay behind when the party is over. I would like a word with you. I'll pay for transport to take you home, if you want."

The Farmer And His Wife

ANNE says I have a naughty sense of humour. I say thank goodness I do, as there seem to be far too many people going about with long faces.

I once heard a doctor at a dinner party expounding on the fact that people who are happy and have a sense of humour will live a long time. Well, I am now over 80 — I think that speaks for itself!

One day, Anne was out and I wanted a word with my son-in-law, Ian, a farmer in Perthshire, about the effect on our way of life and our pockets by a directive from Brussels.

I picked up the phone and was answered by our daughter, Mary.

"Dad, hold on a minute, there's a bird in the kitchen," she told me, and I heard her yelling to her husband.

She was, so I learnt later, trying to make something for a lunch party she was giving the next day. The last thing she wanted was a bird in the kitchen!

When she came back on the phone, I asked, "What type of a bird is it? How did it get in? Is it big enough to cook?"

"Dad, if you have nothing better to say, get off the phone!"

When Anne came home I told her about Mary and her bird in the kitchen, and laughed.

by
John
Taylor

She didn't think it was at all funny, and there and then rang Mary to commiserate. Half an hour later she came off the phone and gave me dog's abuse for my lack of sympathy when Mary was so busy!

You see why my sense of humour gets me into trouble . . .

THINKING about birds, neither Anne nor I can remember how it came about that neither of us had been in the sitting-room for a while, but one day when she went in, Anne called, "John, come here."

There was a dead starling on the floor, and what was worse, a porcelain figure of a

Sharon felt her face turn crimson.

"That won't be necessary, Mr Kirkwood," she said. "But yes, certainly. Of course I'll stay."

SHE went back to stand by the buffet-table, putting on a brave smile. But inwardly she was screwed up with anxiety. Bad enough if the old gentleman had made some complaint there and then. But she felt certain he must have a lot to complain about if he wanted her to stay lady we had been given as a wedding present was in smithereens on the stone hearth.

Our next encounter with an unwanted bird came one evening when we were in the middle of tea.

Anne answered the phone and, after listening for a few minutes, I heard her say, "We'll come up right away, Mary, dear."

When you hear a remark like that you immediately wonder if there's been an accident!

Eventually Anne came off the phone, and I waited for the worst.

"John, would you believe it, a crow has built a nest in Mary's lounge chimney!"

I was so relieved I burst out laughing, but Anne couldn't see anything to laugh at.

Apparently, Mary had invited a few guests for a get-together on the Saturday night. The nights were drawing in and she decided to have a log fire burning.

As they had not had a fire in their lounge all summer, she lit it on the Friday night just to warm up the room. She noted it was going and shut the door.

Half an hour later she looked in and was met by a cloud of smoke. A crow had built a nest in the chimney.

We didn't go to help as Anne had promised, but I know how Mary and Ian spent that Friday night!

Anne and I nearly parted company over a pair of swallows. They built a nest under the eaves just above the dining-room and bedroom windows.

Anne hadn't noticed them building their nest — but soon noticed their droppings on both window-sills. She, houseproud as always, demanded I knock their nest down.

I refused, promising to clean up the mess after the youngsters had flown, and for once I had my way.

Both Anne and I are interested in birds and we derive great pleasure from watching them.

We bought half a dozen tit nesting-boxes from the Forestry Commission at Tentsmuir. They were the type that had hinged lids so that you could see how many eggs were laid.

We managed to site one so that we could watch the birds' comings and goings from the kitchen window.

The day the young decided to leave home, I think Anne spent all her time watching them hover at the wee hole and then take the plunge into the big wide world. She even bought a book solely devoted to blue tits and became an expert on the subject.

Our worry is there are fewer of certain breeds about today compared with the days of our youth. The thrush is declining in number and so are the birds that used to nest on our top fields, such as the plover, the snipe and the corncrake.

Let's hope that some of the breeds we have today will not decline and be seen no more.

behind, especially to hear it.

It was like having to go and see the headmaster after school. She began to think of all the things that might have been at fault. Had the tongue been stringy? Or the biscuits soft? Perhaps they ought not to have made the pastries last night. Had they gone soft?

Mrs McBain was never going to forgive her, if she had lost a customer like Mr Kirkwood at his first function. She might even think it was bad enough to warrant dismissing her. After all, there were plenty of girls with qualifications like hers looking for jobs.

And if I am dismissed, what chance have we of paying off that wretched overdraft? she thought miserably.

Suddenly she became aware that everyone was clapping, and saw that one of the men had lit Mr Kirkwood's birthday-cake, which was sitting on a little table in the centre of the room. The old gentleman stood up and bowed.

"I'm not even going to try to blow out the candles," he told them. "So don't ask me."

Sharon looked round at the happy, laughing faces of the eight well-dressed couples and felt a great pang of envy. Then the party was over and the guests filed out.

"Mr Kirkwood wants me to stay behind and have a word with him," she told Julie and Peter rather self-consciously. "Would you explain to Mrs McBain?"

"Nothing wrong was there?" young Julie asked in alarm. "I didn't do anything, did I, Mrs Bell?"

"Nothing that I saw," said Sharon, trying to sound unconcerned. "In fact I thought you did very well."

AFTER Peter had carried the last of the empty trays out, Sharon could delay the moment of truth no longer. She took a deep breath and walked from the kitchen back into the dining-room, where Mr Kirkwood was waiting for her in his easy-chair.

"Come over and sit down, my dear," he said quietly.

Well, at least he doesn't sound furious, she thought with a certain relief. She did as she was told and waited.

"Well," said Mr Kirkwood, looking at her shrewdly from beneath his brows, "what's the trouble, young lady?"

"I'm sorry?" Sharon asked, blushing.

"You're worried about something," the old man said. "It's been on your mind for the last two hours. Would it help if you talked about it?"

Sharon looked at him in astonishment.

"I don't know . . ." she faltered after a moment.

"Try it," Mr Kirkwood said. Then he leaned over towards her, and his voice became gentler. "Shall I tell you why I asked?" he went on.

"It was because in the whole of that room, you were the only one who looked as if you had a heart. No, let me go on," he said quickly, as Sharon made to speak.

"Those nephews and nieces of mine don't know what life is. They all have too much money. They're always wondering what to spend it on next. I hear the same conversations every time I see them.

"When Muriel, my wife, was alive, we would have a good moan about them after they had gone. She *did* know what living was, you see. We had our ups and downs, I can tell you. That's her there. In the photo on the sideboard. You can tell she had a heart, can't you?"

Sharon looked at the humorous, wrinkled face in the photograph and nodded.

"Actually I would like to talk, Mr Kirkwood," she said quietly. "But it's not a very thrilling tale. Quite run-of-the-mill, I suppose. But it's the worst thing that's happened to me since I was married."

"Make us a pot of tea first," the old man suggested gently. "It's easier to talk over a teacup. Have you never thought so?" His eyes twinkled at her and Sharon found herself smiling back. She was beginning to warm to old Mr Kirkwood more and more.

S HARON told her story between gulps of tea, hiding nothing of her hurt and indignation.

"To think that he could have done that to me!" she finished, tears springing to her eyes.

"Poor chap," Mr Kirkwood said softly.

Sharon thought she was hearing things.

"I beg your pardon?" she said.

"Poor chap," repeated the old man. "He's been a fool. But he loves you, doesn't he? Try to forgive him."

"I can't!" Sharon cried.

Mr Kirkwood sighed heavily.

"My dear," he said, "bring me that photograph over, would you? The one of my wife."

Sharon did so, and the old man tugged at the picture behind the glass with stiff fingers. It slid out eventually and Sharon saw there was another photo beneath it. One of a handsome boy, with "Love from Tim," scrawled along the foot of it.

"Fine lad, wasn't he?" Mr Kirkwood said sadly.

"Was?" Sharon asked sharply.

"He was our son," said Mr Kirkwood. "We lost him when he was eighteen."

"Oh, I'm sorry," Sharon whispered. "Was it an accident?"

"Human frailty. That was what was to blame," the old man said dully.

"Muriel and I had gone on holiday in the June of that year. When we came back we discovered that Tim had taken a sum of money from the petty-cash in our office. It wasn't a great deal. And he had never done it before. He swore he would never do it again. I don't think he would have.

"It had been a stupid impulse. A repair needed to his car which had broken down when he had promised to give some friends a lift. Not a great deal of money, as I say. But it was the deceit that horrified us. The breach of trust. Just like you say you felt this morning. We couldn't forgive him that

"The atmosphere in the house was terrible. Finally I suppose he

WELFORD-ON-AVON, WARWICKSHIRE: J CAMPBELL KERR

couldn't stand it any more. He left home one night in September to hitch-hike south. He was killed by a lorry on the A1."

"Oh, no!" said Sharon, her eyes bright with tears.

"Yes, my dear. And I don't know how many times Muriel and I sat here together and said, 'What was wrong with us? It was only money. Why did we behave as we did? He wasn't a bad boy. He loved us. And we loved him.'

"So try to forgive that husband of yours, my dear. He has been silly. And you will probably find it hard, paying off the money you owe. But don't harden your heart like we did. It's not worth it."

"No," Sharon said. "I see that." She walked across and hugged the old man impulsively. "I can't thank you enough."

"There." Mr Kirkwood chuckled, patting her hand. "None of those celluloid relations of mine would ever give an old man a hug. That's what Muriel and I used to call them . . . 'the celluloid people' . . . wicked, weren't we?

"And if you ever have an evening to spare, you and that young husband of yours . . . or perhaps I wouldn't like him?" he finished doubtfully.

"Oh, you would!" Sharon cried. "He's a lovely lad. He's so good-natured. And he has a marvellous sense of humour."

"You see — you've forgiven him already," Mr Kirkwood pointed out with a mischievous grin. "So you bring him round one evening. We could maybe have a game of cards."

"That would be lovely," Sharon said. "I'll telephone and we'll fix a date."

"Promise?"

"I promise. I'll look forward to it." She was feeling happier than she had done all day, when she left five minutes later.

"There now, Muriel," murmured Mr Kirkwood, smiling down at the photograph on his lap, now replaced in its glass.

"I've made a new friend. Two new friends probably. It hasn't been such a bad birthday after all.

"And maybe I've done a bit of good. Are you smiling? Yes, you are! I knew that you would approve, my dear." ∎

◀ *p.15* # *WELFORD-ON-AVON*

IN a setting as pretty and as picturesque as a chocolate-box lid, Welford-on-Avon in Warwickshire has remained unchanged for centuries.

Its village green is the scene of traditional May Day celebrations, complete with Morris dancing round a maypole which is surmounted by a golden ball and a fox weathervane.

AWKWARDLY buttoning up my coat, I followed Mother outside. She paused for a moment on the doorstep, checking in her shopping bag for her purse and studied its contents carefully.

"Hmmmmm." She snapped it shut, closed the door and set off.

With a hop and a skip, I was soon beside her, reaching up for the warmth of her hand, ready for the adventure. Not for us the ordinary Main Street shopping of bread and tea, and just enough sausages. No, today we were venturing down back streets I wasn't allowed to walk alone.

Today we were going to sample the mysteries of Sophia's Bazaar.

Along the street we went, past the mill with its gaping doors and dim interior of huge, clacking looms and shadowy people. Hidden danger lurked there.

We hurried on across the canal bridge — with a quick, tiptoed scramble to peer at the dark water — and walked on down the long cobbled hill. We turned right. I stepped off the edge of my known world and shrank a little closer to Mother.

Other people must have walked along those streets but I saw only the pale winter sun warming the stone of pavement and wall; long

MUM'S SPECIAL SECRET

By Ruth Stanier

corridors of housing joined at sharp corners, leading us along.

Mother quickened her step. Round the corner we marched and there it was — a large square building with an open oblong doorway and a red-painted sign above announcing "Sophia's Bazaar". There was no pavement and no step up or down so we walked straight inside.

I HAD never seen such a big room. Trestle tables lined each side with busy adults selling from large boxes of neatly-arranged goods.

Mother retrieved her shopping list, eyes searching purposefully.

"Hmmmmm. Yes. Over here." She began to replenish her collection of useful items; shirring elastic and safety pins, two and a half yards of quarter-inch elastic for knickers and garters.

I glanced down at my fawn-clad legs and self-consciously hitched up one wrinkled sock, then hitched up my knickers for good measure before bending again to tuck my home-sewn garter out of sight.

Grandma knitted our winter socks. Sometimes that pleased me, sometimes it didn't.

Mother was already moving on, peering, lifting, handling, discussing the merits of this or that type of fabric with eager saleswomen and fellow customers alike.

Then, "I need some new ticking for the bolster," she announced and headed off across the room.

I dawdled behind, gazing with longing at gleaming white socks in their pristine rows — if only . . . With a sigh, I turned to the next stall.

A wobbly woman, all chins and billowing bulges, was searching through woolly vests. She picked one up. It was much too small. I went round her to find the Liberty Bodices. I liked their curved shaping and tiny buttons. I liked my own. I had it on today.

I meandered onwards and suddenly found myself staring at pink corsets with suspenders on. I looked away and then, glancing to ensure that Mother was still occupied, I sneaked another blushing look.

With a guilty start, I turned around and went to join Mother — but where was she? There were hundreds of mothers milling around, all carrying shopping bags, all wearing sensible shoes.

I couldn't breathe. I couldn't see her. I dodged under elbows, squeezed past coats, panic threatening. Then, blessed relief, I heard her voice.

"Sixpence ha'penny, did you say?"

I went and stood next to her, discovering a sudden interest in the delicate flowers embroidered on handkerchief corners. She looked down.

"Ah, there you are. Good. Let's go and look then."

She pointed to a stall in the corner. We walked over together.

Colour blazed out at us. Best blue velvet snuggled next to shiny green satin. Yellow striped flannel squashed red checked gingham. A whole trayful of ribbons perched atop rolls of flowered curtaining. There was even a box of lace. I touched it with my fingertip and traced the pattern.

Mother went to the very end of the stall.

"Here," she said. I went and I saw, gasped at the glory of it all. Rolls of brightly-coloured netting stood in a rainbow, all wound up and ready to be chosen. "We'll need a fairish amount to make your costume."

I could see it in my mind. I would be the most beautiful girl on the stage — changed in an instant from dumpling to rosebud.

Mother counted out the coins as the woman wrapped the netting in brown paper, twisting the end.

"Would you like to carry it?"

I nodded, took the parcel and held it gently.

NOW," said Mother kindly. "You've been a good girl. Time for your treat."

Another? I trotted behind her. In the centre of the room was a large wooden barrel. Sawdust sprinkled the floor round about.

"It's the Christmas bran tub," explained Mother. "Go on. I've paid."

I dabbled my hand into the sawdust.

"Here," said Mother impatiently. She took my parcel from me. "Dig in properly."

I unfastened my coat and took it off. Giving it to Mother, I pushed up my sleeves and then delved both hands deep into the barrel. The sawdust felt gritty between my fingers.

I leaned hard until I was elbow deep. I scrabbled my fingers around feeling mysterious lumps. This one, that one, a round one, an edgy cornered one; which should I choose?

My fingers bumped against a long, thin parcel. I twisted to grasp hold of it, pulling it carefully towards the surface. The sawdust mountain erupted as my hands and parcel appeared. A fine film clung to my arms like sand at the beach.

"Open it then."

I shook the remaining grains from my present and peeled back the wrapping paper.

There were three pencils. They were colouring pencils; one red, one blue and one yellow. The red was rosy, the blue like the sky. The yellow one was almost gold. I held them up and twizzled them round.

Then I noticed. There was writing on them; a name. G-R-A-C-E; Grace. It wasn't my name. It wasn't my present. It was just any old thing, something someone else hadn't wanted. I blinked back tears and went to hide the pencils in my pocket.

"Here," said Mother. "Give those to me."

I did as I was told.

She turned them over, saw the name and frowned. For a long minute

Morning Birds

FROM a tree in the woods,
As the night grows grey,
A pigeon's soft croon
Greets the coming of day.

Hundreds of rooks,
A black noisy crowd,
Harshly cawing, fly past
To fields newly-ploughed.

In the garden a robin
Chirps his refrain,
Praising a world
Refreshed by the rain.

In a pear tree the thrush
His song has begun,
Greeting with rapture
The red rising sun.
— Berta Lawrence.

she stared, and then she smiled down at me.

"Well, fancy that. Father chose your name, but if I had chosen I would have called you Grace. It can be your special name. A secret just for you and me." She handed the pencils back.

I gazed in wonder. My own secret special name and it was written on my present. I beamed up at Mother.

"Come along then," she said. "Home time."

We left Sophia's Bazaar. Mother carried all the useful things she had bought. I carried my rosebud material and my special, secret-name colouring pencils.

At the corner of the street I stopped and looked back at the red-painted sign over the oblong doorway. Suddenly I knew.

"When I grow up big," I declared loudly, "I'm going to have a bazaar. I'm going to have one and it will be just as exciting as Sophia's Bazaar."

I turned to Mother. She was already half way down the street.

"Wait for me," I called and ran to join her. ∎

T HERE you are. Bright and cheerful, those flowers are. They'll bring a bit of sunshine into the ward, won't they?" Maimie Dunlop smiled as she handed over the colourful bouquet. This was a grand wee job. She was so grateful to her neighbour for spotting the advertisement.

Not that it was permanent. Poor Mrs McGinnis, the lady who normally looked after the hospital flower stall, had broken her leg. Maimie was just standing in for her — literally — until she was fit again.

By Karen E. McAulay

Maimie loved chatting to the visitors who stopped to buy flowers for a patient — or, as was often the case, for the nursing staff. Sometimes her customers looked so

SAY IT WITH FLOWERS

anxious that she made a special effort to cheer them up. Few people failed to respond to her easy-going banter.

Maimie was a born extrovert; the life and soul of any party. Her daily routine was punctuated with little chats over the garden wall, or with neighbours, or at the shops — with anyone who happened to cross her path.

The only problem was that she sometimes didn't know when to stop. And whereas it didn't matter quite so much if she inadvertently put her foot in it with friends, she realised only too well that she had to be extremely tactful with her customers.

"Talk to them, by all means," Mrs McGinnis had told her, "but don't keep asking how the patient is. If they want to tell you, that's fine, but sometimes they'd rather not talk about it."

Maimie blushed slightly as she remembered a couple of occasions when she'd forgotten this advice, and ended up uncharacteristically lost for words. Still, she'd learned her lesson now.

TAKE the young man she'd served half an hour ago, for example. He came to the hospital every day, and was one of her best customers. He bought flowers at least twice, if not three times, a week.

"They're for a very special person," he'd said, the first time he came in. "She can't see very well, but she can make out bright colours . . ."

"And how's . . . ?" Maimie had asked him, the next time she saw him. He'd shaken his head sadly.

"No change," he replied. His face had what Maimie would have described as a closed look, and she didn't question him further.

Still, she had to admit there was as much happiness as sadness in this job. Babies were born, people got better, nurses earned well-deserved thanks. The only kind of celebration she hadn't been involved in was a wedding!

Now, that would be a real challenge. How many flowers would it take to fill the hospital chapel?

Her daydream was broken by a pleasant young voice just behind her.

"I'd like a pot-plant of some sort," said the girl. "For an old gentleman to take home with him. We'd better choose something that'll be easy to look after."

Now, here was someone who'd enjoy a chat, Maimie sensed.

"Does he live on his own?" she asked conversationally.

"As a matter of fact, he does," the girl answered.

Now Maimie came to look at her more closely, she realised that the girl was probably older than she looked. It was her small height that was deceptive. Maybe she was the old gentleman's daughter?

"But you'll be looking in on him, of course?" Maimie prompted.

"Oh, yes. But he's got plenty of friends and neighbours, too. They'll help him." She winked. "And water his plants, I hope!"

They chose a beautiful big pot of chrysanthemums. Maimie's customer declared herself well pleased.

"Yes, that's exactly what I had in mind. Well, keep up the good work — er — I'm sorry, I don't know your name . . . ?"

"Maimie Dunlop."

"You're doing a grand job, Maimie. The wards look lovely, and most of those bouquets are thanks to you. 'Bye for now!"

What a pleasant young woman, Maimie reflected. She didn't expect recognition for what she did, but it was nice to receive the occasional compliment.

She'd grown to recognise the regular visitors — like the sad young man — but she didn't recall seeing that girl before. And yet, with her auburn hair and green eyes she was distinctive, to say the least. Maybe the old man had only been in hospital for a short spell.

Maimie loved to make up stories about different people. Take the old man, for example. Had he been ill? Or had broken a limb? And *was* the young woman old enough to be his daughter?

And the sad young man? Was he visiting his wife? Or his mother?

Maimie felt so sorry for him — not to mention the lady whose eyesight was failing. How terrible, to look across the room and not be able to tell the difference between roses and peonies, or daffodils and tulips!

A S the days went by, Maimie's customers came and went. The auburn-haired young woman rushed past on several occasions, waving cheerfully as she hurried along the corridor. She didn't stop to buy flowers, or have a chat, and Maimie wondered if the old man was maybe making a slower recovery than expected.

The sad young man seemed to grow more dejected every day. Maimie longed to hug the drooping shoulders, or take him across to the tea-bar for a cup of hot chocolate. He looked as though he could do with the chance to unburden himself.

But she knew her place was with her flowers — not to mention the cash-register! Whether he noticed the extra flowers or sprigs of pretty foliage that she slipped in was neither here nor there. It was her way of showing that she sympathised.

He was standing making his choice one evening, when a familiar cheery voice made him turn round with a start.

"Duncan McDuff! I haven't seen you for ages! Not since college, in fact. What are you doing here?"

Maimie envied the girl her easy familiarity, as she squeezed the young man's hand warmly. Her green eyes were alight with pleasure.

"Do you remember Annie?" Duncan managed a tired smile. "She was the year behind us at college? Anyway, it's a long story, but there was an accident. She's been in here three months already, and I'm afraid it seems that she has taken a turn for the worse . . ."

"Oh, the poor girl! Could I visit her? Or would it be too much for her?"

"I'm sure she'd be delighted to see you, Rachel."

Duncan fished in his pocket for some money to pay Maimie for the flowers. He hardly glanced in her direction as he picked up his bouquet and left the stall with Rachel.

Half an hour after, Maimie was pleased to see Duncan and Rachel coming back along the corridor together. She nodded approvingly as Rachel led the way into the tea-bar.

It'll do him good to talk to someone, Maimie reflected. I know how worried you must feel, Duncan, but you really shouldn't bottle it all up.

She quite often saw them together after that. But funnily enough, although she'd initially been pleased to see Duncan enjoy a good blether, Maimie began to feel distinctly uneasy as the days turned into weeks. A perceptible warmth was developing between the two young people.

When she saw Rachel lean forward across the table and hold Duncan's hand, it was all Maimie could do not to go across and say something.

"Just look at that!" she whispered to Mrs McGinnis, who had come in to say that she'd soon be fit for work again. "Those two have both got sick relatives upstairs! I'm sure that boy is married and she visits an old man I presume is her father . . ."

"You and your imagination, Maimie!" Mrs McGinnis laughed. "I don't suppose you know anything about them, do you? What makes you think the lad is married? Does he wear a ring?"

"I — well, I'm not sure," Maimie demurred. "But he visits someone about his own age, every single day. If she's not his wife, she's a very serious girlfriend. They've known each other since they were at college together.

"But this girl holding his hand — Rachel — she's a *nice* girl. How could she be so unfair to a friend?"

Mrs McGinnis dismissed the subject with a wave of her hand.

"Why don't you just forget it? They're young — they've got their own lives to lead. They don't need complete strangers worrying about their personal affairs . . ."

Maimie let her ramble on. She was feeling a little low after hearing Mrs McGinnis's news. Only another fortnight, and then it would be back to the little flat that had been her home for so many years. It would seem lonely after working here at the hospital . . .

WHEN it came to her last week, Maimie decided to make a special effort to be cheerful, for the sake of all her customers.

"Hello — it's me again!" came Rachel's familiar voice. "I think I'd

FERRY TALES

Aberdour to Inchcolm (Firth of Forth)

by Colin Gibson

Inchcolm Abbey

I must confess I am happier on land than on the sea in a small boat.

But, with friendly tides and a gentle west wind touching our faces like velvet, my shipmates and I had every chance to enjoy the ferry crossing from Aberdour to Inchcolm --- the Isle of the Dove or Columba's Isle.

Also called sometimes the "Iona of the East", it lies 1½ miles from the north shores of the Firth of Forth, and it welcomed us with sandy bays and pastures that were less grass than a mosaic of tiny flowers, still dewy with morning mist.

The venerable abbey, partly in ruin but now well cared for, was a delight to visit. The roofed buildings include the domestic ranges and the cloister arcade which has a series of windows with window-seats --- quite charming in its effect.

My sketch shows the square bell-tower and the unique octagonal chapterhouse.

Inchcolm Abbey was founded by Alexander I in return for the kindness shown to him when he took refuge on the island in stormy weather. Like Iona, it became a holy place, "near to heaven".

Gone for ever are those early men of the Christian Church, but it seemed to me that, in spirit, they must still be here on this lovely Isle of the Dove.

---

like some more chrysanthemums. The bigger and brighter the better!"

"For the old gentleman again?" Maimie eyed her suspiciously. "He's been here a good while longer than you expected, hasn't he? Is he definitely being discharged today?"

Rachel burst into laughter.

"Heavens, no — they're not for Bob this time! He's been home for ages. No, these are for Duncan's girlfriend. She's . . ."

She broke off as Duncan came in behind her. Dropping her bag, she held out both hands to Duncan, and kissed his cheek impetuously.

Maimie thought she'd explode with a mixture of anger and curiosity.

"Hey, you two!" she burst out, her cheeks a fiery red and her grey curls bobbing furiously. "What are you thinking of? What about Duncan's Annie? You should be ashamed of yourselves!"

Duncan and Rachel stared at her, stunned into silence.

Now the harsh words had been spoken, Maimie was already regretting her outburst. So much for all Mrs McGinnis's advice! Oh, why didn't I keep my mouth shut?

"I'm sorry," she began hastily. "I'm just an interfering old fool. I should have . . ."

Why were Duncan and Rachel smiling at each other in that extraordinary way? Maimie couldn't decide if they looked more perplexed or amused. They certainly didn't look cross.

"Why, Maimie, what *is* the matter?" Rachel asked. "You must have got the wrong end of the stick. Maybe I'm to blame — I'm just a naturally demonstrative person. But I'm not a scarlet woman — if that's what you're thinking."

Duncan wasn't smiling. He was beaming broadly.

"Oh, Maimie, what a muddle!" he spluttered. "I've been coming here so long, and I've been so preoccupied. If I'd been a bit more talkative, you wouldn't have dreamed up such a hilarious fantasy . . ."

He paused to pull a hankie out of his pocket, and wiped his eyes. A little box fell from the folds of his hankie, and he stooped to retrieve it.

"This —" he grinned, opening it to show her "— is an engagement ring. Annie was in a bad car crash some months ago. Her eyesight will never be the same again, but it's gradually improving. She insisted she didn't want to be a burden, though I told her I'd love her no matter what.

"Anyway, yesterday was the happiest day of my life. She's agreed to marry me at last!"

STILL confused, Maimie looked searchingly at him, and then at his companion.

"And you, Rachel? Are you happy for them?" she whispered cautiously.

"Happy? I'm ecstatic! The hours I've spent trying to persuade Annie that she and Duncan are made for one another . . ."

"You've been visiting Annie all this time?"

Rachel's face dimpled as she chuckled mischievously.

"Annie, and a lot of other people." She nodded. "I'm a minister. Sick-visiting is part of my job. But I'm very pleased . . . No, *you* tell her, Duncan!"

"Rachel has promised she'll perform the wedding ceremony just as soon as it can be arranged. In the hospital chapel, no less. You will arrange the flowers, won't you?"

Maimie grinned broadly.

"The regular flower lady will be coming back next week — I've just been a temporary fill-in. But it'll be more work than she could cope with on her own, won't it?"

Duncan and Rachel nodded solemnly.

"Much too much for one person," Rachel agreed.

"Then I shall be pleased to oblige. It'll be an honour!"

Impetuously, she flung an arm round each of them.

"Oh, what a lovely finish to my working life!" ■

WHEN they arrived, Roger found a note stuck to Grandpa's front door.

In greenhouse.

"Plants, in this weather!" he muttered under his breath. "You stay here," he said to the boy, "and I'll go and fetch him."

Thomas glowered under his fringe as the gleaming shoes disappeared briskly around the side of the house. Yesterday's thin covering of snow was crisp as a wafer, and his father's footprints were sharp and businesslike.

SUCH PRECIOUS MOMENTS

This was the last place in the world Thomas wanted to be. He hauled his bag of clothes half-heartedly to the front door, and squinted at the note. He recognised Grandpa's spidery writing from last week's birthday card:

Have a nice time. I wish I was seven again!

Love Grandpa.

The picture was only trees and bluebells. Thomas had pulled a face and stood it behind the dinosaur cards from his friends. Now, he ripped the note off the door and began to tear at the paper irritably, feeding the tiny pieces to the sharp wind. He didn't notice his father reappear.

"Thomas! What do you think you're doing?" Impatience

By Dawn Gorman

chiselled deep lines between Roger's eyebrows.

Thomas stared at the path between them in silence.

"I asked you a question," Roger repeated, glancing at his watch as though timing his son's silence.

In fact, the gesture was pure habit. Since setting up his own electronics company, there were so many demands on Roger's time that he now automatically guarded every minute against unnecessary wastage.

Tension mounted as father and son stared at each other. Then suddenly, they both heard the steady clump of wellingtons, and as Grandpa appeared around the corner of the house, Roger turned instead to him.

"Don't know what's wrong with Thomas at the moment, Dad. Hope he doesn't give you too much trouble."

Grandpa rested clear blue eyes on Thomas, then smiled calmly.

"Don't you worry about us, Roger," he said in a careful, even tone. "Now, will you have a drink before you go?"

"No time for that, I'm afraid. The flight goes in three hours. It's a shame Sue's had to go into hospital now, and Thomas is missing a week's school, but I've got to wrap up this Geneva deal."

He spoke quickly, as though his words were already stacked in businesslike order inside his mouth, ready for use.

"Now you behave yourself," he cautioned Thomas, hurriedly ruffling the boy's hair. "I'll be back a week today." He walked briskly to the car, and leapt inside. With a last wave, he drove off up the road.

THE two watching figures stood quietly for a moment. Grandpa broke the silence.

"Come on then, Thomas, let's have a nice hot drink to warm us up, eh? Then you can help me in the greenhouse."

Thomas followed his grandpa reluctantly. He didn't know him well. Roger's business commitments often extended into the weekends, and there never seemed to be enough time to make the eighty-mile trip to see Grandpa. Even when they did manage to squeeze in a visit, they never stayed for long.

Roger found it difficult to relax, and his father's slow, methodical ways made him even more impatient to be up and away.

In the kitchen, Thomas sat with folded arms and watched as his grandpa made him a hot orange drink, then spooned tea into a round brown teapot. An old wooden clock filled the silence with its loud, steady tick. It seemed to slow everything down to its own, measured pace.

"So, your mam's in hospital, then?" Grandpa said finally.

Thomas chewed the skin on the side of his thumb, but said nothing. The old man produced a sponge cake and carefully cut two slices. As

Thomas reached for his, he looked up at his grandpa, and his eyes suddenly filled with tears.

"The baby's not going to come until next month . . . she could be there for weeks, and I'm stuck here," he mumbled, his voice ending in a sob.

Grandpa gently put his hand over Thomas's. At first, Thomas wanted to pull away, but the gentle pressure somehow started to make him feel safe, and the warmth felt like the sun on a June afternoon, so he didn't move.

"It's just to make sure everything's all right this time," Grandpa said. "Your dad *has* explained, hasn't he?"

"Not really," Thomas said with a sniff. "He just said it would do her good."

"I think your dad's a bit too worried to get his thoughts straight at the moment," Grandpa began gently as he poured the tea. "Do you remember when your mam was having a baby last time?"

Thomas nodded solemnly.

"Well, something went wrong, and the baby died before it was born." Grandpa poured milk in his tea, choosing his words carefully for the child.

"So this time," he continued, "as soon as your mam's blood pressure went up, they wanted her to stay in hospital so they could help."

"But what if . . ." Thomas couldn't find the words to describe his fears.

"She'll be all right, don't you worry. The baby as well. Now, eat your cake, we've got some gardening to do."

THEY spent an hour in the greenhouse every day. At first, Thomas stared out at the snow, sulky as a goldfish in a bowl. Every so often, he jumped up and down to get warm.

"What do we have to keep coming in here for?" he demanded on the second day. "It's freezing and I'm bored."

"Well," began his grandpa, "big jobs seem smaller if you do a bit every day." He held out his hand to Thomas. "Do you know what these are?" he asked.

Thomas took a cursory glance at the pale flakes in the outstretched palm.

"No," he answered.

"They're tomato seeds."

"Are they?" Thomas's amazement was out before he could stop himself.

"They're not like that when they squirt out on to your jumper, are they?"

"No," Thomas murmured, trying to sound uninterested, although Grandpa noticed with amusement the boy's sidelong glances at the sowing procedure when he thought he wasn't looking.

"Come on, you do these," Grandpa ventured.

Thomas was soon engrossed. Following his grandpa's instructions, he filled a plastic tray with compost, drew out four shallow drills with a stick, and carefully placed seeds in each. When they were covered up, he looked at his grandpa expectantly.

"What happens now?"

"Now we have to find a space for them in the kitchen, keep them damp, and wait."

"Just wait?"

"That's right. You can't rush nature."

The next morning, the snow had melted, and Grandpa showed Thomas the rest of the garden. Under the bare cherry tree by the drive, they spotted some new, dark green leaves.

"What are they, Grandpa?" Thomas asked.

"Ah, they're snowdrops. They come up regular as clockwork every January, no matter how cold it is. See the buds? They'll be in flower soon."

At the end of the week, however, the buds were still tight little parcels. Thomas had just been out to check them when the telephone rang.

His grandpa was still outside and didn't come when he shouted, so he answered it himself. When the old man returned, Thomas called him into the hall.

"Grandpa!" he whooped, his eyes wide with delight. "It's Mummy on the phone and she's all right and the baby's come and I've got a sister!"

"Well, a little lass. That's grand! Can I have a word with your mam?"

Thomas jumped up and down excitedly, and only caught the odd snatch of what Grandpa said to his mother. "He's been a good lad . . . I just wish . . . stay again."

Later, Thomas wanted to put some snowdrops in a pot for Mummy. Grandpa smiled at his eager face.

"Well, they don't really like being disturbed when they're going to flower. How about setting some seeds for her instead?"

"But they'd take ages to grow," Thomas pouted. "It'd just look like a boring old pot of compost."

"Ah, but if you explain that they're flower seeds, she'll know they're worth waiting for."

THE next morning, Thomas's bag stood ready packed by the front door, a small plant pot next to it. He was so excited about going home, he couldn't eat his breakfast.

"Does Daddy know about the baby, Grandpa?" he asked suddenly.

"Yes, your mam managed to call him in Geneva."

"I can't wait to see Mummy. And the baby."

"What about your dad?"

"Not him," he said, staring at the table. "He doesn't talk to me like you do. He just rushes around and says, 'Not now, Thomas'."

"He loves you too, Thomas. But it's hard for him. He's so busy he's just run off his feet," said Grandpa. "Anyway, listen to this. How would you like to come back at Easter and talk some more? Your tomato plants will be ready to set out in the greenhouse then."

"Can I? Really?" Thomas began, but his excitement was punctuated by the beep of a car horn. "He's here!"

Roger came in though he was obviously eager to be off again. While Thomas hopped around impatiently at the open front door, he spoke to his father.

"Thanks for doing this — I really do appreciate it," he said, patting the older man's shoulder.

"It's been no trouble at all. He's a good lad . . ."

"No problems, then?"

" 'Course not. He appreciates it when you spend time with him, explain things to him."

"Really?" Roger said, pausing for a moment in surprise. "Well, that's good. You must have the magic touch. Anyway, we must get off."

"Roger." His father reached out to grip his arm. "I know it's not easy, but try to give the boy a little of your time."

Roger sighed, then nodded.

"I'll try." He picked up Thomas's bag and took it to the car.

THOMAS followed carefully with his pot of flower seeds, his breath making clouds in the cold air. Suddenly, he noticed a tiny, white umbrella under the cherry tree.

"Look, one's come out!" he shouted excitedly, turning to look back at his grandpa. Grandpa smiled, and Thomas suddenly felt an uncontrollable surge of happiness. He carefully put down the pot on the drive and ran back to hug the old man.

For a moment the two stood motionless while Roger watched from the car.

"Now, remember about Easter, won't you?" Grandpa said finally. "I asked your mam on the phone yesterday, and she said it'd be all right."

"Great!" whispered Thomas conspiratorially.

He was so happy when he climbed into the car that he flashed an unexpected grin at his father. To his amazement, his father smiled back and something about the crinkles around his eyes reminded Thomas of Grandpa.

He sat down contentedly, the pot of seeds held safely on his lap. He thought about Easter all the way home. It seemed a long way off, but it would be worth waiting for.■

ARE you all right up there?" Helen stood at the bottom of the ladder and peered up into the gloom of the loft. The noises were really rather alarming, and she was afraid John might put his foot through the ceiling at any moment.

"Yes, I'm OK. I'm not having any success, though."

John's voice was faint as it drifted into the rafters above him.

"Shall I come up and help?" Helen asked reluctantly.

"If you like," John said, "although I know it's not your favourite place."

He reached down and helped her up the last of the steps on to the loft floor. Although there were two lights, it was still gloomy and the corners were dark.

"How shall we ever find anything in all this?" Helen asked. "Why did we keep so much rubbish?"

She lowered herself carefully on to a square of pink carpet.

"Like this, for instance. What's it doing here?"

John laughed. "That was when we had a pink nursery for Josie."

"But that's nearly twenty-five years ago," she protested. "I know you don't like throwing anything away, but this is ridiculous!"

"We can't all be as unsentimental and clear-headed and efficient as you, darling," John said, as he sat down beside her. "Some of us love our old things and keep them near us instead of taking them off to the council dump! I'm nervous that you might do that with me one day soon!"

They laughed as they sat in the gloom and surveyed the unwanted contents of the loft after thirty-five years in the same house. They had set out to look for their son's rowing photographs, and that was proving to be a problem.

Matt and Katharine had been married for two years, and had just moved from a tiny flat to a small house with a large garden farther out in the country. They had room now for all

32

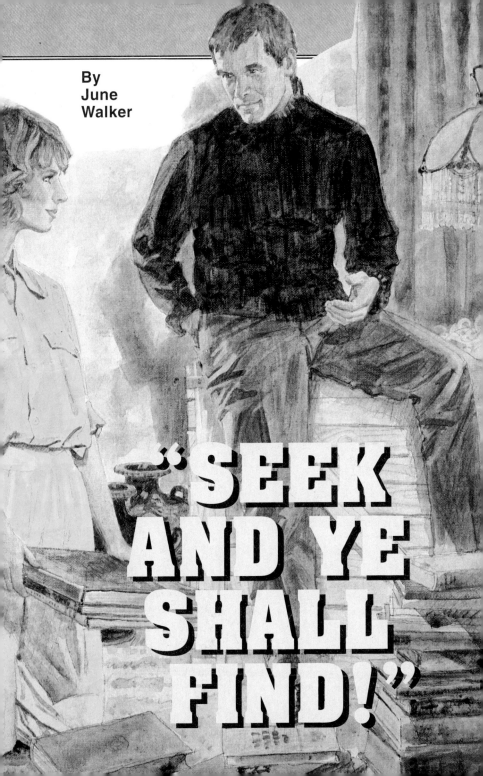

By
June
Walker

"SEEK AND YE SHALL FIND!"

their possessions, and could commute into London quite easily.

After spending a day with his parents a few weeks before, the young couple had managed to clear most of Matt's junk, apart from several boxes of miniature cars and soldiers. They had happily climbed up and down the ladder staggering under boxes, filling Helen's bin liners, and finally managing to squeeze everything into their small car to make just the one journey home with it all.

But Matt couldn't find his photographs. They were mounted and ready to hang, and understandably he was upset at their loss.

John decided he would have another look and he had already spent an unsuccessful half-hour moving cases, boxes and furniture in the hope of finding them.

Now he said to Helen, "You're quite right — there's too much stuff up here. I didn't realise quite how much we'd stowed away. When Josie has taken what she wants, we'll tidy it all up so that coming up here isn't such a chore."

Josie, eight years younger than Matt, had moved out to share a flat with two friends and was anxious to have some of the old furniture, rugs and lampshades until she had enough money to buy new.

Helen and John had just retired, and were looking forward to a more leisurely life now that they were on their own.

"I'm not getting very far with this," John admitted. "I'm sure they're here somewhere. I'll have a look in that far corner."

Walking carefully across the boards, he vanished into the gloom. Helen stayed where she was listening nervously to the shuffles and bumps. Re-emerging into the circle of light, John put down a large cardboard box.

"I think they're in here. But look what I found in the corner."

He put something into Helen's hands.

"I remember that!" she exclaimed. "That's Mother's old camera. I wonder how it got over there."

"Well, let's go downstairs now and check the photos — it's too dark to see anything up here."

In the kitchen, John removed the lid from the box and there were Matt's photographs, vibrant and colourful with scarcely a trace of dust.

Then he examined the old camera.

"This still has a film in it," he said.

"It would be fun to see what's on it," Helen suggested. "Will it be any good after all this time?"

"We could take it to old Mr Parkinson at the Station Pharmacy," John decided. "He must have seen plenty of films like this over the years."

The following morning he took the old film in to Mr Parkinson.

The old man stared.

"I haven't seen one of these for years," he said with a smile. "I suppose you want to see what's on it."

"Is it possible?" John asked. "Can it still be processed?"

Mr Parkinson rubbed his chin. "I can send it to the laboratory with a note that it's very old and asking for special care to be taken with it. They'll probably ask advice from the manufacturers, so it will take longer than usual to process it.

"And I can't say exactly what the cost will be," he warned.

"That doesn't matter," John told him. "My wife's very keen to see what's on it. We don't mind paying a bit more."

THAT evening Helen rang Matt to let him know they had found his treasured photographs and would bring them across when they came to see the new house in a few weeks' time.

Matt's interest in them had waned considerably, however, as he and Katharine had some exciting news — they would be parents in the late summer!

Almost before Helen and John could take in the news, Matt expounded on how important it was these days for grandparents to bond with their grandchildren. There were even special grandparent classes if Helen and John felt like going along!

"You wouldn't mind baby-sitting, Mum, would you?" he asked. "And perhaps having it for the odd weekend now and again, or while we go on holiday sometimes?"

Helen listened to her son with a mixture of love and impatience. He had never been a boy to use tact or discretion, she thought, as she struggled with an almost overwhelming depression. She tried hard to be enthusiastic, and John added his congratulations, but as she put the phone down she realised that at this moment she did not feel like becoming a grandmother.

Looking up, she met John's eyes.

"Is there something wrong with me?" Her voice trembled and John put his arms round her.

"I know I'm going to be thrilled about the baby, but I was looking forward to spending some time on our own. We've both worked so hard at our jobs and bringing up the children, and now it seems that Matt wants us to look after the baby while he and Katharine carry on with their lives as usual."

John kissed her.

"Now, Helen, let's be sensible. Matt was carried away with his news and he was tactless as usual — and I'm sure he was only joking, anyway.

"He knows quite well we're too far away to be called on too often — and look how long it takes us with all the roadworks on the motorway now. We'll do our bit when the time comes, but we'll lead our own lives, too. Don't worry about it."

"Katharine is going to have to take Matt in hand and see that he's more tactful," Helen said. "He just doesn't think."

"Just the way you did with me, remember?"

Helen laughed. They were so alike, father and son, in looks and character. But I wouldn't change either of them, she thought with a rush of love.

"You'll see," John went on. "He's just over-excited at the news — he'll calm down soon enough."

The following week they collected the snaps from Mr Parkinson. The colours were muted but all five pictures were clear, showing an elderly man in the garden with a small, dark-haired, laughing boy.

"That's Matt, with Dad!" Helen exclaimed! "They were planting the cherry trees. Matt was only about six — I remember those little blue shorts."

Grandpa had an enormous spade and Matt was holding his tiny one with a flourish.

"Look at the trees now," John commented as they opened the patio doors on to the garden. "I can hardly remember them being small. So how old exactly is this film?"

"Twenty-eight years," Helen said promptly. "We didn't have Josie then. When she came along, I used to stand her pram by the trees."

THEY had thought Matt was to be an only child, and then when he was eight Josie was born. At first Matt thought he was losing face to have a tiny baby sister, but very soon he adjusted to her and had proved himself a wonderful older brother. They had been good chums right through their lives and kept constantly in touch.

Helen looked at the little snaps time and time again. She had almost forgotten those carefree summer days when the children were small and life seemed so gentle.

John watched her carefully and realised that she was gradually coming round to thinking about the new baby with warmth and pleasure.

One evening they were sitting surrounded by cruise brochures when the phone rang. When Helen answered it she heard her daughter-in-law's voice at the other end.

"Helen," she began, "I've been up to visit Dad for a few days, otherwise I would have rung you before. I wasn't here when you rang and Matt told you about the baby."

"Katharine, dear, we're so thrilled for you," Helen broke in.

"Yes, I know you are, but Matt really shouldn't have given the news and then immediately talked about baby-sitting and so on. He said you didn't sound exactly over the moon and I'm not surprised! In fact, I've given him a good dressing-down," she added mischievously.

Helen laughed. "They're both the same, father and son. I had to work on John for years to make him think before he spoke, and Matt is just

Snowman

*B*UILT *by two schoolboys'*
Willing hands,
Out in the garden
The snowman stands.

Jack Frost stays with him
All through the night,
And decks him all over
With diamonds bright.

Clad in white armour
When darkness is done,
Glittering, dazzling,
He faces the sun.

— Berta Lawrence

the same. They just blurt out what's on their minds.

"Anyway, we're delighted we're going to be grandparents. I hope you're not going to do too much over the next few months."

"I'll stay on at work for a bit, but I'll find the commuting tiring, I imagine. Anyway, I wanted to say a big thanks for finding Matt's photographs. I don't think he even bothered to thank you for doing that, he was so excited about the baby.

"Will you have time to come across and see us at the weekend and bring them with you? I think you'll like the house, and we're going to hang the photos in the dining-room."

Then John came to the phone. He was fond of his daughter-in-law and wanted to have a word with her. Then he and Helen returned to their brochures.

Helen said thoughtfully, "I've been in my office in an adult environment for too long. I've forgotten what it's like to have small children around."

"Well, you'll soon find out again!" John warned her with a laugh. "But let's make up our minds on our cruise. I vote we go in early summer, so that we're around later on when the baby arrives."

"That's a splendid idea," Helen agreed.

She stole another glance at the little snaps on the table beside her.

"I'm so glad we found that old camera in the loft," she murmured. "It's good to be reminded of the pleasures of a family." ∎

HILDA lowered herself into the deckchair and eased off her shoes. She let out a sigh of pleasure. It was good to get the weight off her feet.

After a while, she took a compact out of her bag and studied herself critically. Her hair could do with another rinse — the sun was showing up where the grey came through the blonde. She powdered her face and touched up her lips.

"Well, Hilda," she said out loud. "You're no oil painting, but

DANCING DOWN THE YEARS

you're not bad for seventy-five."

The sun was warm. She would concentrate on the match in a minute. She wasn't really interested in bowls, but it didn't look right not to give support.

The sounds of the summer afternoon soothed and relaxed her. She heard the gentle click of the bowls, the muted consultation of the players and the scrape of a hoe as a gardener nearby weeded a border.

He was whistling as he worked. That tune — what was it? Oh, yes, of course. *She'll Be Coming Round The Mountain*. They'd been playing it that night in 1942 when she'd met Dave at the ENSA dance. She hadn't been fat then — far from it.

**By
Robyn
Johns**

She hadn't been Hilda Lorraine either, come to that. She'd just completed her training and she was ACW Blackett. She'd been slim as a reed and luckier than most because the WAAF uniform had suited her — even the hat . . .

AN Army corporal took her ticket and held the blackout curtain to one side.

After the darkness of the night, Hilda stood just inside the hall, bemused by the lights. She'd just been posted and she didn't know anyone yet. But she wasn't worried. Her short career in the theatre had cured her of being shy with

strangers. It had done her the world of good.

The smoke-filled room was packed with RAF and Army personnel, all shuffling round to the beat of the band. She looked round, wondering which of these big hunks would be the first to ask her to dance.

Hilda felt a tap on her shoulder, turned round and there he was.

Some hunk, she thought. He was about as tall as she was. But he was smiling broadly and she couldn't help smiling back.

"You're looking a bit lost, love," he said. "Come and have a dance."

The band was playing *She'll Be Coming Round The Mountain* as a quickstep and Dave had whirled her energetically into the middle of the floor. He seemed much too young to be a Flight Sergeant. The regulation haircut made him look like a boy but his insignia showed him to be a gunner.

He had deep blue eyes which sparkled as he looked round the hall.

"You've saved my bacon," he said with a grin. "That's what you've done!"

"Glad to be of service, I'm sure," Hilda replied demurely. "What have I done exactly?"

"Well, just take a took round! ATS, WAAFs and WRENs by the score and every one of them taller than me! Sometimes I feel a proper half pint, I can tell you. To tell the truth, I was feeling a bit homesick just then and wishing I was back in Ilford. Then all of a sudden there you were — just my style!"

"Ilford?" Hilda was looking at him in disbelief. "You don't come from Ilford, do you? Well, I never — so do I!"

"There you are then," he said. "We're meant — you and me. I knew it the moment I saw you."

It felt like that to Hilda, too. They danced the whole evening together and afterwards he walked her back to her billet.

"You're a smashing little dancer," he said. "Did anyone ever tell you?"

"Lots of people," Hilda laughed. "And so I should be, considering I was a pro before I came into this little lot."

He stopped in surprise.

"A pro?"

"Yes. I've been dancing ever since I was a kiddie. My first paid job was in panto at the Ilford Hippodrome."

"Go on," said Dave. "Which one?"

"*Aladdin.* With Maidie Summers."

"I don't believe it! I saw that."

"Well, you saw me then, because I was in the chorus. I've been in the West End, too. Did you ever hear of a show called *The Girl From Brazil*?"

"I'll say. I saw it with my mum and dad. It was a fantastic show.

You're not telling me you were in that, too?"

"I was. Only in the chorus, of course. But I had a couple of lines — in the shop scene where we danced on the counter."

"Well, I'm blowed!" Dave shook his head in amazement. "Fancy me watching you in the theatre and not knowing it — and now here I am walking you home!"

THEY saw as much of each other as their duties allowed. They went to all the dances and the sing-alongs in the local pub. They sang *Roll Out The Barrel* and *Bless 'em All,* Dave always singing louder than anyone else with a pint glass in his hand and an arm clamped firmly round her waist.

They watched Betty Grable and Alice Faye in the camp cinema and rode borrowed bikes in the Cumberland lanes. It was all so comfortable and so right. Falling in love for Hilda was like coming home and putting on a familiar pair of slippers.

Dave was sent down south after that. He became a tail gunner in a Lancaster and Hilda was worried.

"You will take care, Dave?" she said. "I couldn't bear it if anything happened to you."

He caught her up and swung her round.

"Don't you worry about me," he said with a laugh. "I was born under a lucky star. I found you, didn't I? If that doesn't prove it, I don't know what does. Get this straight, Hilda, my old darling — nothing is going to stop us being together when this is all over. Nothing!"

And miraculously, it didn't.

After the war, Dave went back to being a plumber. He started to make good money and he didn't see why they shouldn't get married right away.

"There's no hurry, is there?" Hilda said. "To be honest, I wouldn't mind having another crack at show business before I settle down and you land me with six kids."

Dave was content. As long as she was happy — so was he.

"But how will you get a job?" he said. "You've been away from it since before the war."

"We'll just have to see, won't we? But I've got plenty of push, though I say it myself. And I've still got some contacts."

She went back to daily dance classes, changed her name from Hilda Blackett to Hilda Lorraine and eventually went to an audition, landing herself a job in the chorus of an American musical about to open in London.

Dave waited for her in the pub near the stage door, every bit as nervous and excited as she was.

"Guess what?" Her eyes were alight with triumph. "They asked me to read and sing as well as dance and they've only gone and offered me the understudy to one of the principals! What about that? Not that I'll get a chance to go on. I've heard all about her. She'd drag herself on with crutches before she'd let anyone else have a go."

The show ran for a long time and Hilda revelled in the familiar atmosphere of the theatre. That was like coming home, too. She loved the backstage gossip, the excitement and the laughs. She forgot all about the WAAFs and the war and seemed completely happy.

She and Dave didn't discuss marriage any more, but she was fiercely loyal to him just the same.

Other girls in the company dated actors or dancers or rich guys they met socially, but Hilda wanted none of that.

She had Dave. He was there, the backbone of her life and she took him for granted like the air she breathed.

Then fate intervened.

THE girl she was understudying got pregnant and was forced to leave the show. The part was passed temporarily to Hilda but to everyone's surprise she made a hit. She had a big voice and a big personality, and the audience responded to her so well that the management told her she could keep the part.

Dave was over the moon and he came to see her nearly every night, until Hilda told him he'd be better off mending burst pipes.

"But I like watching you," he said staunchly. "When you come on I want to stand up and tell everyone you're my girl."

Then, one night, a smoothly-dressed man in a belted camel boat knocked on her dressing-room door. He said he was a talent scout from an American film studio and asked her if she was prepared to meet some studio executives for lunch on the following day.

"Pull the other one!" Hilda laughed in his face as she scrubbed her make-up off with a towel. "I didn't fall off a Christmas tree, thanks very much!"

She really did think someone was having her on. But the man produced his card and the next day she went off to the Savoy in a new hat, spent two hilarious hours with the producers and agreed to have a film test.

"Although what they want with my ugly mug I can't think," she said to Dave that night.

"They know a good thing when they see it," Dave replied. "That's what they're paid for."

If she hadn't been so excited, Hilda might have noticed he was less enthusiastic than he'd been over her previous successes.

The film test was made at the British studios of the film company. Apparently, it was satisfactory because, like a bolt from the blue, she was offered a trip to the States and the option to sign a seven-year contract. She was beside herself.

FERRY TALES

Sligachan (Skye) to Raasay

by Colin Gibson

Nowadays, there is a good ferry service from Skye to the island of Raasay, and well do I know that crossing! I drew and painted it often when, for two summers, I accompanied as artist the expeditions sent out by Dundee University to explore the biology, botany and geology of the Inner Hebrides.

At that time, I may add, the ferry-boat was rather different --- it was only a small boat with an outboard motor which started (hopefully) with the help of a piece of string!

But the surrounding scenery of the Red Hills and rugged escarpments were just as they are now -- truly magnificent.

Raasay is quite historic, linked, for instance, with Bonnie Prince Charlie and also with those unlikely 18th century tourists, Dr Johnson and James Boswell, who thoroughly enjoyed themselves here.

Boswell, with Young McLeod of Raasay and others, climbed the highest hill, Dun Caan, and, exhilarated by the climb (and a glass of whisky), they danced a reel on the summit.

So, not to be outdone, and strictly to keep up the tradition, you understand, my party of research students, plus the artist himself, did likewise!

"I just can't believe it," she said. "I know things like that have happened before — that's how they got Greer Garson. But me? Little Hilda Blackett from Ilford going to Hollywood! Just think — I might meet Clark Gable and Fred Astaire. Shall I give your love to Lana Turner?"

"So you'll really go?" Dave looked bewildered. "It's wonderful for you, of course." He was trying his hardest to look pleased for her, but he couldn't quite manage it.

Hilda came down to earth with a bump. It was the first time she'd faced the thought of leaving him.

"What are we to do, Dave?" she cried. "I don't want anything to come between us, but how can I turn my back on a chance like this?"

"It puts me in a proper pickle and no mistake," he said. "I don't know if I should be fighting to keep you or if I should stand back and let you go."

"Oh, well," said Hilda. "I haven't gone yet and I expect something will happen to stop me."

But it didn't.

The London office of the studio stepped in with a vengeance and Hilda Lorraine was "taken in hand".

She was given elocution lessons to make her London accent less noticeable. Her teeth were re-modelled, her hair was bleached and re-styled. Then they told her that her name wasn't suitable so they changed that, too.

"Blimey!" said Hilda, slipping back to her roots without thinking. "Cara Lamont! I ask you!" She studied her new image in the mirror. "Dave! What have they done to me?"

"You look — very nice," he said doubtfully. "Not exactly my Hilda — but you look good enough to be on the films, all right."

He sat glumly on the sofa. It was clear he knew she was passing out of his reach.

SHE was to sail on the Queen Elizabeth. It was all getting very near and Hilda was beginning to feel trapped. She looked at Dave, loving him with a hollow ache in her stomach. He was so unchangingly loyal.

She loved his bright, astute eyes. She loved the way his short hair made his ears look endearingly large.

She knew now she didn't want to go, but she was caught up in a relentless machine and seemed to have no choice.

Dave took her to the boat train and stood awkwardly among the rich, successful travellers. Hilda by now was almost unrecognisable in a fur coat, two rows of pearls and a hat with a spray of dark feathers framing her face.

"You don't half look expensive," Dave told her with an attempt at humour.

"Nothing but the best for Cara-blooming-Lamont!" Hilda tried to laugh but nothing came out.

The train began to move and Dave stood on the platform watching it go. Hilda hung out of the carriage, waving.

Then suddenly she leaned much farther out. She tore her hat off and waved it frantically, shouting something that Dave couldn't hear.

He ran after the train but it was going too fast and he had to give up. He watched while it took Hilda away and out of his life.

THE sound of applause brought her back to the present. The bowls match was over. Hilda opened her eyes and saw Dave walking towards her in his blazer and white flannels.

"You've never been asleep?" he asked accusingly.

"I only closed my eyes for a moment," she said. "Did you win?"

"You bet. We licked 'em hollow."

"Just as well you did." Hilda heaved herself out of the deckchair. "Considering we've spent the whole afternoon here instead of at home getting everything ready for the party."

She slipped her arm through his and looked at him fondly. He hadn't really changed. His hair still grew like it did when he was in the RAF. It was grey now, of course, but at least he had kept it.

He was still alert, still quick on his feet with the same twinkle in his eyes.

"I've been thinking about how we were," she said.

"I knew you weren't watching the match."

"It's funny, though. When you're young you think you know exactly what you want — then when you get older you find out you didn't really want it at all!

"Just think, if I'd gone to the States, I wouldn't be here now. I'd probably be a scrawny old has-been living on memories in some New York apartment. Ugh!"

Dave grinned at her.

"No-one could call you scrawny now!"

"I know." Hilda said contentedly. "It was marrying you that did it. And having the kids. But when you first met me you could get your hands to meet round my waist, remember?"

"Yeah, and I couldn't get the garden hose to meet round it now." He gave her a squeeze. "But I like you better this way."

They walked on in silence.

"The only thing I'm sorry about," Dave said at last, "is that I wasn't there to see you zooming down the ship's gangway, just as they were trying to take it away!"

"Talk about in the nick of time." Hilda laughed. "I didn't even wait to see the boat go. I was off like a rocket and on the first train back to dear old London. Ha! You should have seen your face when I turned up at your place that night."

"I'm not surprised. I thought I was seeing a ghost. It was pouring with rain and you didn't have a hat or coat."

"I left them on the ship. They weren't mine anyway. They belonged to somebody I couldn't be."

"No regrets then?"

"What? After all this time? Don't be so daft. Mind you, I'm not saying I haven't wondered what it would have been like. But then I think of our Joanie and Pete and Billy and our Freda and I know I did the right thing."

Dave gave her a hug and kissed her.

"Of course you did!"

"Here! Watch it — you saucy monkey. Anyone would think it was our first anniversary instead of our forty-sixth!

"Talking of which, if we don't get a move on we'll have the whole family, grandchildren and all, arriving home with not a table laid and a sandwich cut . . ."

"Oh, well," said Dave. "The show must go on . . ." ∎

JENNY gazed at the blue, swirl-patterned lounge carpet covered in felt-tip pens and pieces of cut-up sheet. It had seemed such a simple idea in the beginning, but now she was wondering why on earth she had bothered.

This never had been her kind of thing. Exhausted, she let out a long, drawn-out sigh.

"Muu-uum," Thomas whined, picking at the sides of his ghostly costume. "This is coming apart at the seams."

"So's mine," Ben groaned, adding insult to injury. "Why couldn't *Dad* do it? I bet he's making costumes for someone *else's* kids."

"That's enough, Ben!" Jenny snapped. "You know he's not with anyone else's children — he's just moved in with your gran for a while."

Taking note of her tone she paused, aware that the core of her anger stemmed from herself and no-one else. She knew it wasn't fair of her to take it out on the boys.

The Magic Of Love

By
Julie
Goodall

"Look, I know he's better at this," she told them gently, "but I'm doing the best I can."

She fiddled unconvincingly with the seams. "What time is Mrs Harris coming round?"

As she spoke, the doorbell rang out in reply.

"Oh, no, she's already here! You go, Ben! I'll just pin this up," she mumbled, pins between her lips. "Thomas, you'll have to be careful, OK?" she told him, slipping them hurriedly into the seams.

The lounge door opened and she glanced up to discover her neighbour dressed as a witch.

"Hi, Jane — almost ready. Now you two do as Mrs Harris tells you. How many have you got, Jane?"

"Nine little monsters."

"Rather you than me! Right, you're off. Now be careful, and . . ."

"*We know*!" the boys chorused.

The front door slammed as a grinning Jane was practically dragged outside, one boy on each arm, the sounds echoing through the quiet house for a few moments.

Then Jenny was left alone with the silence that followed and the pop of a few early fireworks exploding intermittently in the distance.

Flopping wearily into the armchair, she placed her head in her hands, resting her eyes and allowing herself some much needed time to reflect on the events of the past few days.

The difficulties had been gradually building up, she realised, but neither she nor Brad had managed to cope with them before their final row.

She was aware, too, that the rows might not have happened had Brad not been given his first contract to work away. It had been a good one, too, meaning extra money for Christmas. Jenny could remember clearly when he had returned home from work one Monday evening with a hesitant look in his eyes.

The firm had chosen him for a trial period of testing sales in the north, with a view to expanding its southern-based stationery business.

Jenny had known it was recognised throughout the office that Brad had done well to be the man who was selected, and combined with his hesitant look had been a definite hint of pride.

BUT four months of his travelling backwards and forwards had taken its toll on them both.

In retrospect, she couldn't believe she had ever been quite so childish, but having become used to her own company and her own way of doing things over the weeks, there had begun the stirrings of resentment when he had returned home every weekend. Previously insignificant matters had started to get on her nerves.

Take the laundry, for instance, which had remained a minor bone of contention since the very start of their married life together.

Jenny's idea of dealing with clothes ready for washing was usually to put them in the basket perched conveniently at the top of the stairs. Brad's method had always been to file them untidily on the bedroom floor.

On his arrival home every Friday, Jenny would empty her husband's suitcase and see to its contents, deciding whether or not the items were in any need of attention.

If not, she would fold them up neatly and repack them in time for when he would leave.

Nevertheless, every Sunday evening after he'd gone, Jenny would gather up the socks, pants and tee-shirts that had accumulated by the bedside cabinet at the weekend.

Somehow, after five days of living in a totally mess-free zone, Jenny found this more irksome than when she had lived with the untidiness every day.

"Can't you just pick them up?!" she'd snapped one Sunday morning whilst vacuuming round the bed. "It's not difficult, is it? Why is it so impossible for you to do?"

In her temper, she'd thrown two pairs of his socks and pants out of the bedroom window and on to the newly-cut front lawn.

Brad had sauntered across to the window and peered out, highly amused.

"What did you do that for?" he'd asked, turning towards her, his blue eyes filled with mischief as he attempted to keep a straight face. "You know freshly-mown grass makes me sneeze. And you've just given poor old Mrs Ranton a heart attack — she was walking past with that rat of a dog."

Despite his intentions, Brad's smoothly handsome features had broken into a smile.

"Well, she's not the only one with a rat," Jenny had muttered, half-wishing her voice hadn't been drowned out by the noise of the vacuum cleaner as she had made her way into the hall.

Why did he always have to treat everything so light-heartedly? She knew she could get too worked-up about some things, but Brad never took anything seriously. All he would do would be to make fun of her and laugh.

Then there had been the matter of the football stickers all over the house. With two boys, Jenny had long given up hope of any resistance when it came to the topic of sport. It was on TV, all over their rooms and creeping into every conversation. But those football stickers and the albums had been the last straw.

"They're everywhere I go!" she'd complained, stepping over the ones which Thomas had spread out all over the bathroom carpet to look at, at the same time as brushing his teeth.

"I'm fed-up with tidying up — it's all I ever seem to do! And you're no help," she'd told Brad forcefully, ignoring that teasing glint in his eyes. "You encourage them. Fancy letting them look at their sticker books in the bath!"

"Jenny, they're only kids." He'd sighed, attempting to slip his hand into hers and give it a squeeze. "You're only young once and all that. You really should try to lighten up."

"Yes, well perhaps I could if I didn't have to look after these two all week on my own and go to work. And, besides, I'd only intended having two children," Jenny had continued, gathering two handfuls of stickers. "Instead, I seem to have ended up having three!"

Tired and exasperated, she had tossed the offending items into a drawer in each boy's room.

Of course, after each falling-out, she and Brad had made up quite happily. Then one Friday, everything had been different. They'd had a major bust-up over the dishes, but no making-up had ensured.

JENNY'S ranting had turned to horror as Brad had thrown his now well-used suitcase violently into the car. He'd only been home a couple of hours, but Jenny had already emptied his suitcase and placed his dirty clothes in the washing-machine.

This time, Jenny realised, she'd pushed Brad too far.

Why, oh why, couldn't he have seen that she needed him to give the boys some discipline once in a while? Had he been right when he'd said that the children needed a balance?

She was rather strict with them herself, she had to admit. Perhaps a little leniency from their father was required to even things up.

Jenny supposed that, if she were honest, he didn't let them get away with *too* much.

BAMBURGH CASTLE, NORTHUMBERLAND

BAMBURGH Castle in Northumberland has existed in one form or another for over 1400 years.

Originally the seat of the kings of Northumbria, the castle was extensively restored and extended in the 18th century, when it was acquired by the Trustees of Lord Crewe, the Bishop of Durham. At the end of the century it was used as a boarding house to train servant girls, as a surgery and dispensary for the poor and as a haven for shipwrecked sailors.

Lord Armstrong, the arms tycoon, bought Bamburgh Castle in 1894 and restored it to form the Armstrong family home.

BAMBURGH CASTLE, NORTHUMBERLAND : J CAMPBELL KERR

Had he also been right when he'd asked why it mattered if the dishes were left to dry by the sink? Just because she had become used to drying and putting them away when Brad had been away didn't mean to say that they had to be put away when he was home.

"We should be making the most of our time together," he'd told her, quite sensibly she realised in retrospect. "We hardly see anything of each other. I don't want to waste time that I could be spending with my family tidying up my socks!"

With a sinking heart, Jenny had to admit that he'd made a good point. She had been so busy worrying about the housework, she hadn't allowed herself to relax and enjoy Brad when he had been home.

The poor man didn't *want* to be working so hard, away from the boys and herself all the week. After all, he rang home early every evening to speak to each of them.

All she had done was to think about how hard it had been for her.

Suddenly, Jenny wanted desperately to hold him and tell him how sorry she was. The empty room only emphasised how much she needed him to be there, even to make fun of her, and maybe to tell her to lighten up. She knew that his cheeky grin would eradicate in an instant the hollowness that she now felt.

FOOTSTEPS sounded on the path and, distractedly, Jenny reached for the box of sweets she always kept at hand for the children on Hallowe'en. Switching on the hall light, she opened the door on to the night.

A tall, dark-cloaked figure faced her, with two little peak-hatted wizards at his side. The man wore a mask across his eyes, and the child on his right squeaked his message with a stifled laugh.

"Trick or treat!" the wizard gasped.

Jenny's grip on the door handle grew tight.

"Thomas?"

The small head bobbed up and down in reply.

Amazed, Jenny looked at the wonderful costumes Brad must have made for the boys. She could see Jane loitering with the other children at the gate.

Straining her eyes, she felt certain she could make out that tatty, battered old suitcase . . .

"Brad, is this some kind of trick? Because if it is, it's not very funny . . ."

Her indignant voice was silenced by the blue eyes gazing down at her from the mask. They seemed to have regained their sparkle after the angry blaze they had possessed four nights earlier.

The tall, cloaked figure stepped forward, drawing her into his arms, the mask moving slowly closer until Brad's warm mouth covered hers.

Closing her eyes, Jenny could almost believe that the last three months were merely a nightmare. At last, she heard an embarrassed giggle from the boys on the step.

"Why aren't you in Birmingham or somewhere, at work?" she asked, astounded, as they reluctantly ended their kiss. "Shouldn't you have gone back on Sunday? They'll have been expecting you..."

Brad pulled her protectively close.

"I rang in sick — I had to get myself sorted out," he whispered, so that the two boys couldn't hear. "I couldn't have gone back to work feeling like this."

Taking Jenny's hand, Brad placed it over his heart.

"See, it's empty." He smiled. "It needs refilling before I go back. If you want me to go back, that is. Tom could take over the trials if that's what you really want."

Speechless, Jenny shook her head.

"Look. I know I've been very selfish," Brad went on, touching her flushed cheek with the back of his hand. "Just arriving home at weekends, expecting you to wait on me hand and foot after a week looking after the kids.

"Perhaps I should have made more of an effort — brought home some flowers, helped some more with the housework."

"Oh, Brad, it wasn't all your fault." Jenny sighed. "You haven't changed — it was me. Everything has been getting on top of me. It wasn't that I couldn't cope, but . . . well, I suppose I just resented you being away. I missed you."

A warm finger rested lightly on her lips.

"Perhaps we ought to forgive each other," he interrupted, "that is, if you can put up with my socks by the side of the bed."

Smiling, Jenny took her hand from his chest and gently squeezed his, closing her eyes to forestall the tears that had welled in her eyes.

"I'll tell you what." She grinned, happily accepting a peck on the cheek. "I'll try to lighten up if you do your best to locate the linen basket. And we'll leave the draining-board cluttered at the weekends, until you're home during the week."

"It's a deal!" Brad cried, shaking her hand with a laugh.

Behind him, realising all was now well and impatient for the sweets they knew were held in their mother's free hand, the boys began to jump noisily inside the front door. The matter they were concerned with was their question of Trick or Treat.

"Treat! Treat! Treat!" they chorused, excitedly.

Brad, still holding their mother, turned towards their two sons.

"You go ahead," he said, taking the sweets from Jenny's hand and smiling wryly as he passed them to Thomas. "I think mine and your mum's is yet to come." ■

MARJORY TAYLOR drew the last dustsheet over the last counter in the store and sighed with relief. Miss Torrance called her staff together. There was only Norma McGill, Marjory herself and young Cathy the junior, but Miss Torrance addressed them as though she were General Montgomery before El Alamein.

"Ladies, we now have three days' holiday, but I stress that our sale begins immediately after that, and I look for you all to appear no later than seven-thirty in the morning on that day. Ahem, and a Happy New Year to all of you."

With that, they were free to go, having worked an hour extra in preparation for the January sale.

McKissocks was not the largest department store in Dundee, but it was undoubtedly "high class". Marjory was grateful for her job in such an establishment, though, in "Ladies Modes", Miss Torrance's discipline, which amounted at times to tyranny, could be something of a strain. On a normal day it was trying, but this had been no normal day. It was Hogmanay.

It was not even a normal Hogmanay, but the last day of 1949. A new decade, in fact, a new half century, was only six hours away as the girls crowded into the tiny staff room.

Norma, whose defence against the "poshness" of McKissocks was to use local dialect whenever possible, flopped into the only chair, kicked her shoes off, and declared, "Meh feet's killing me, roll on June."

She was getting married in June to a joiner who worked with Marjory's father out at a new

A GUID NEW YEAR

housing estate at Downfield. When Marjory had inquired, her dad had said, "Oh aye, nice laddie but no' that bright." Not an opinion to pass on, especially since Marjory was to be bridesmaid!

Young Cathy threw her coat on and called, "Happy New Year when it comes."

"The Square tonight, Cath?" shouted Norma, but Cathy had already dived through the door, glad that Miss Torrance could not make her life a misery for at least the next three days.

Now, Marjory could still remember when she was fifteen years of age, and just out of school, as Cathy was. It wasn't easy, but you settled in and began to realise that Miss Torrance wasn't quite so bad. Well, when you'd stuck it for five years as Marjory had, it didn't seem so anyway.

"Square tonight, Madge? First-footing and so on?" asked Norma.

Marjory replied that she didn't think so. The family were gathering at her house this year, and her mother would need all the help she could get. The truth was that Marjory did not care for the New Year too much.

Outside the store, the High Street and along the Nethergate was a hive of activity, as stalls were being erected for the sale of red herrings dressed in crêpe paper, and other traditional first-footing gifts.

The Overgate was

by James Christie

crowded with people, and, no doubt, the buster stalls were already in the full flow of business along in Mid Kirk Style. Norma and her fiancé were going to Franchi's restaurant for high tea, having to queue to get in, without doubt.

Marjory decided that she was quite glad to be heading for Shore Terrace and the bus home. At least, when you worked late the bus was less crowded.

MARJORY quite enjoyed her bus journey to and from work. In fact, she did most of her thinking during those fifteen-minute voyages! This evening, there was an air of excitement, since Hogmanay parties and the holiday stretched ahead, and Marjory had to concede that it was difficult not to feel caught up in it all.

Living in Dundee, she could not admit to anyone that she did not care for New Year, because it would be regarded as a form of blasphemy, or at the very least, unpatriotic!

But there was something in her nature which made her look backwards with sadness when the bells rang out, rather than forwards with anticipation or any feeling calling for celebration.

Marjory could remember only too well the first time she was allowed to stay up till midnight on Hogmanay, at the age of ten. When Big Ben boomed from the wireless, and everyone exclaimed "All the best", and began shaking hands and kissing, she dissolved in tears.

To her lasting embarrassment, she became part of family tradition. Grandad's bald head turned a strange puce colour after two drinks of what he called "Nelson's Blood", Cousin Isobel played "The Wedding of the Painted Doll" on the piano, Uncle Bob bellowed "Steady the Black Watch" at frequent intervals, and young Madge had a good "greet".

The single-decked bus swung round a corner, and Marjory noticed lights still on in Smith & Horners. Preparing for their sale as well, she supposed, smiling inwardly as she thought of Miss Torrance's words — "McKissocks sale is genuine and genteel, unlike the others."

The bus made alarming grinding noises as it struggled up the Hilltown, as though protesting that, having fought its way up past the Infirmary, this was asking just a bit too much.

Reaching the top of the Hilltown, there was not too far to go. Marjory lived with her parents and younger sister, Sylvie, in an upstairs, two-roomed, council house at what they always called "the back of the Law"

Her father had often teased the girls by saying that, if only one of them had been a boy, the family would have been able to apply for a three-roomed house. They all knew, though, that they were lucky to have a council house at all, and luckier still that it was a happy home.

Sylvie was the "bright" one of the family and, at sixteen, was doing a five-year course at school, hoping for "Highers" and a place at university. That did not prevent her from spending a lot of time in what Marjory thought of as "dreamland", and caused her mother to worry about her being "laddie daft". Only a few days ago, Marjory had enjoyed Sylvie doing her Vivien Leigh impersonation while graciously accepting a pound of mince from the apprentice in the Co-op butchers.

MARJORY jumped from the bus, calling back "Same to you!" to the conductor, who had wished her all the best for 1950, and hurried up the road towards home, aware that the others would be awaiting her arrival before starting the evening meal. It was a fine, if cold, night for anyone going first-footing, she thought.

Two bounds up the outside steps, through the door, sharp left, then up the inside stairs. The smell of home at the end of the day. Nobody could describe it.

Her mother was standing over the cooker in the kitchenette at the top of the stairs, with the smell indicating stovies for tea. That, mixed with furniture polish, "Zebo," from the warm grate in the living-room, plus a whiff of her father's Capstan Full Strength, should have been appalling, but it was not. It was home, and it smelt lovely.

"Tea's nearly ready, Madge," called her mother as she checked the progress of the stovies. "Oh, by the way . . ."

Marjory knew from experience, that when her Mum said, "By the way," that something, frequently unpleasant, was about to be announced. Her mother continued, speaking quickly, (another bad sign from Marjory's point of view).

"We have a guest for tea, Tommy Carr, Mrs McGill's grandson from Yorkshire. He's in the RAF at Leuchars. I met him at the hospital this afternoon while visiting, and he wants to see a typical Scottish New Year, so I told him that you and Sylvie would take him to the Square tonight. But you get him back quickly, mind, because I want him for my first-foot."

"Mum, you know I hate the Square, with all the crowds and noise and everything," Marjory protested. Her mother looked at her with a half smile, taking her arm and propelling her towards the living-room, saying, "Anyhow, come and meet him."

In the living-room, Marjory saw first her father, in his usual chair by the fireside. On the settee there was Sylvie, in her best frock.

From alongside her, there was, uncoiling to a height of something over six feet, a young man in an Air Force uniform, who smiled shyly and looked almost as awkward as Marjory felt. Her hair all over the place, McKissocks' regulation white blouse and black skirt making her feel utterly dowdy, as she realised, at a glance, why her mother wanted Tommy Carr to be their "first-foot". He was tall, dark, handsome and also a stranger — just perfect!

The Farmer And His Wife

IT'S — let me check on the wall clock — yes, 3.45 a.m. I'm sitting at our kitchen table in my pyjamas. The stove is on so I'm cosy.

I haven't been sleeping well lately, waking up between two and three in the morning.

About three months ago, I was so worried that I went to my doctor and told him my problem.

"John, you need to lose weight and walk more," he said bluntly. "Here's six sleeping pills."

I hadn't mentioned to Anne that I was thinking of going to the doctor, but I told her about my visit when I got home.

"I would have gone with you, if I'd known, John."

I know she meant well, but I'm 80 and quite capable of stating my own problems to a doctor!

I took one of the sleeping tablets, but never again. I didn't wake up till after nine o'clock in the morning, and when I did I was befuddled.

There are two lamps over our bed, one at Anne's side and one at mine, but I don't like switching mine on to read at 3.00 a.m. as it wakes Anne.

I also have an ancient radio on the wee table by the side of the bed. I can switch it on and listen to the World Service or whatever, but again that wakens Anne.

Rather than toss and turn and wake Anne, I try to ease myself quietly out of bed and, without putting on the light, I go into the kitchen where I am now.

Marjory wished she had time to change, but a quick dash to the bathroom, frantic brushing of hair, and some hastily applied lipstick had to suffice.

TEA was a huge success. Tommy was quiet, but good company. He enjoyed his meal, delighting everyone by asking for a second helping of "stovies". How could anybody live to the age of 21 and never have heard of, or tasted stovies before?

He spoke of his family and his home near Hull and Marjory decided that Tommy was very nice indeed. He even laughed when her father proclaimed that Raich Carter was not fit to lace Billy Steel's boots. Marjory knew little about football, but was sure that Tommy displayed very good manners!

Even Sylvie switched roles to become Petula Clark playing the kid sister, which pleased Marjory, and made her feel more confident.

by John Taylor

Then I sit and read for a while.

TONIGHT — sorry, this morning — I thought I would sit and pour out my problem to you. I can just hear some of you asking why we don't have single beds so that I could toss, turn, read or listen to the radio without disturbing Anne.

It must be twenty or more years ago that we were in a Dundee furniture shop looking for a special wedding present. Somehow Anne managed to lead me into the bedding section where an assistant came forward.

"Can I help you, Madam?"

"I'd like to see some single beds."

"Who for?" I asked.

"Us, dear."

I took her arm and ushered her out of the shop, then I exploded.

She was all for a double bed when we were married, I reminded her. What had come over her? A couple who sleep in single beds is taking the first step to divorce, in my opinion.

I don't think we spoke between Dundee and St Andrews!

"I'm sorry, John, I wasn't really serious," Anne murmured eventually.

Let me explain to you how we sleep in bed. If you are standing at the bottom of the bed, Anne is on the left side nearest the window and I am on the right, nearest the door. She sleeps looking towards the window and I cuddle up behind her.

We've done that for over fifty years. Single beds? Not likely!

Oh dear, I'm in trouble. I can hear Anne's footsteps down our wooden stairs.

"John, are you all right?"

She rubs her eyes as she comes through the door.

"Yes, dear. I couldn't sleep so thought I would tell my problem to the readers."

"We'll put the kettle on and have a cup of tea."

Does tea, at about 4.30 a.m., keep you awake? I'll know tomorrow — no, sorry — today . . .

After the meal, Mrs Taylor took charge. Tommy offered to help with the washing up, but was firmly refused. Mum and Sylvie to the dishes, Madge to get changed were the orders — there was a lot to do before people started arriving.

Getting changed was not easy, since the bedroom was already set up with card tables creaking with shortbread, black bun, and bridies which would later be warmed in the oven.

Marjory was standing, trying to make up her mind between the two possible dresses she could wear, when the door began to open and a deep voice said, "Excuse me, luv."

Panic, which caused her to bump a table and send several pieces of shortbread crashing to the floor, turned to anger, as Sylvie bounced into the room, flopping on her bed, giggling with delight at the success of her prank, before skipping to the door again, and, suddenly solemn, saying, "He's nice, and he likes you, Madge."

There was now a burst of almost feverish activity. Best clean cloth on the table, glasses to polish, the sideboard to be arranged with various bottles, so that it looked as though there were more than was actually the case. A dozen things to do, and re-do, then check again.

Through all this activity, the two men sat talking by the fire, with Jimmy Shand playing, quietly as yet, on the gramophone.

While having a final flail around with the Ewbank sweeper, Marjory heard Tommy gently teasing her father about living in a house full of women.

Dad laughed, and replied, "Sometimes I get annoyed if I walk in the kitchen and get smacked in the face by a wet stocking hanging from the pulley, but there's not a thing I would change." Good old Dad.

Oh, dear, thought Marjory. Three hours to go and I'm getting chicken-hearted already.

It seemed that always, on Hogmanay, there were periods when time stood still, or at least dragged its feet, then everything happened at once.

Gran and Grandad arrived, having taken a taxi. This was a very rare event, and, as they climbed the stairs, Grandad was complaining about the cost while Gran accused him of being a miser. After fifty years of marriage they were almost like a music hall act at times.

Uncle Bob, along with Cousin Isobel, appeared shortly afterwards. Isobel asked how the piano was. Well, the piano was there, behind the settee, looking terrible. Especially since Marjory's father had "modernised" it by removing the fixtures which had been designed to contain candles.

The hole left in the frame did little for the instrument's appearance, nor for its tone, come to that, thought Marjory. However, there was no doubt that Isobel would produce her masterpiece as she always did!

Uncle Bob had been buried by a shell during the war, and was known throughout the family as "Pair Boab." As well as a pension, he was employed in the shipyard but nobody was quite sure what he actually did there. Marjory had long suspected that Uncle Bob was by no means as daft as people thought he was.

THEN Sylvie's friends stormed in, chattering excitedly, with the girls giggling at everything the boys said. Marjory noticed Tommy looking at them with dismay, so delayed putting her coat on as long as possible, so that the younger gang set off a little earlier on their way to the City Square, leaving the other two to follow.

At first, as they walked up towards the shoulder of the Law Hill, it was a little awkward. Then Tommy asked if she preferred to be called "Madge" or "Marjory", and she answered that she was always "Madge" at home but "Marjory" at work, which she really liked better.

"OK," said Tommy, "You're Marjory, and I'm Tom, if you don't mind. This is scarcely a time for formality."

They both laughed, from then on talking easily as they walked. Tom was a draughtsman, but was being trained as a radar operator during his National Service in the RAF, of which he had nine months to do.

They reached the place where the road to the top of the Law curved off into the darkness to their right, and, from here, the route into town was past the High Kirk, downhill all the way. Tom stopped, looking up at the shape of the hill, with the war memorial on top, standing darkly against the starlit sky.

"It must be a tremendous view from up there." He spoke quietly. "You know, I'm not a great one for crowds, so would you mind if we went up to the top instead?"

Marjory's heart leapt. Would she mind?

As they set off up the hill, it seemed quite natural that Tom should take her hand. The lights of the town slowly spread out around them, twinkling lights from Invergowrie to Broughty Ferry, lights stretching in for two miles from the river towards the Sidlaw Hills. Lights across the expanse of the river, in Fife, Wormit, Newport and Tayport, with the railway bridge linking the two shores like a ribbon of black across the water, which shone pale between the two.

On the summit, walking round the war memorial, they looked northwards together, picking out the street where Marjory lived and the school she had attended.

"They say the town will soon reach right to the Sidlaws."

"Who are 'they', Marjory?"

"Well, my Dad, actually."

They laughed together, and moved back round the memorial, to stare out over the bulk of the town and the river beyond.

Marjory had peered at her watch, almost nervously, several times, since it seemed to have frozen at five minutes to midnight. Suddenly, a rocket shot up from somewhere around Baxter Park, they could hear a muffled roar from the centre of town, and sirens began howling from three jute ships down in the harbour.

"It's 1950, Marjory Taylor. Happy New Year." They hugged each other, while Marjory mumbled, her face against the rough Air Force greatcoat, with a brass button hurting her nose, "All the best, Tom Carr."

FROM then on, everything became hilarious and crazy. In order to be sure that Tom would be the Taylors' "first foot", Marjory suggested that they ignore the road, running down the north side of the hill to her home.

The long, tussocky grass was wet, and they slid and skidded their way down, laughing and yelling like children. On the road again, clinging to each other, Marjory was aware that her feet were soaking and she had almost certainly ruined her shoes, but it didn't seem to matter.

They ran to the Taylors' gate, rushing round to the back green in order to raid the Duncans' outside bunker for a piece of coal, so that Tom would be suitably equipped as a "first-foot", and just made it to the door ahead of the Gibsons from downstairs. Marjory's mother was delighted!

"The Wedding of the Painted Doll" was played to great applause. Her Dad sang "Bonny Strathyre" rather well, in spite of being accompanied by Isobel on the piano. Grandad, bald head suitably coloured, recited a poem which owed a lot to Rudyard Kipling, but was entitled "You're A Better Man Than I Am, Dungarees."

Sylvie appeared with a youth in tow. He wore a duffel coat, had a boil plaster on his neck, and was clearly infatuated, which was not too surprising, considering that Sylvie was doing an excellent Lana Turner.

The only time Tom took his hand from Marjory's arm was to salute smartly every time Uncle Bob bellowed, "Steady the Black Watch", which seemed to delight everybody. Mum busied about, looking worried, asking if everyone had enough to eat and drink.

It was New Year and Marjory was loving every minute of it.

Around three o'clock, when the party was still in full swing and Tom was telling Sylvie's youth about the new jets he'd seen at Leuchars, Marjory took a moment to steal away, to lean on the lobby banister and enjoy the rush of cool air from outside.

The door opened behind her and her father joined her. His eyes twinkled as he looked at her and asked, "Happy this year, Madge?"

She leaned over to kiss his cheek.

"It's the nicest New Year ever, Dad," she said.

"I could see that." He squeezed her shoulder. "Many of them, lass. Many of them."

Marjory could never have explained it, but there seemed to be only one thing left to do.

There, out in the lobby, just a few hours into the New Year, she had a good "greet". ■

CALEDONIAN CANAL, HIGHLAND

*K*NOWN *as the "longest short-cut" in Britain, the Caledonian Canal runs in a straight diagonal from Corpach to the Moray Firth, passing through 29 locks and Lochs Lochy, Oich and Ness. It was built to save fishermen and sailors risking their lives in the hazardous waters of the Pentland Firth. Designed by Telford, the canal was started on in 1805. It opened in 1822, but wasn't completely finished until 1847 — at a cost of £1,311,270. Our picture shows the canal at the top of Neptune's Staircase near Lochaber.*

CALEDONIAN CANAL, HIGHLAND : J CAMPBELL KERR

AMY TOWNSEND turned the corner into Blossomfield Road and braced herself against the icy wind. She was glad Mrs Kemp had decided to close the flower shop half an hour early. She'd be home before her son, Iain, for once, and she could start cooking the chops she'd bought during her lunch hour.

Apart from the weather, it had been a good day. This morning Mrs Kemp had appeared with a huge box of daffodils which Amy had arranged in a green tub in the centre of the window. Of course, they'd sold out within a couple of hours.

What was it about daffodils? Every single customer had left the shop smiling. They'd all agreed that although it was only January, spring was just around the corner.

By the time she reached her front gate, snow was beginning to fall, and her fingers were numb as she fumbled for her key.

Several letters lay behind the door, and she picked them up resignedly. They wouldn't be for her.

Really, it was too bad! This was the second time this week she'd had mail for Peter Hamilton. That new postman was an idiot.

She laid the letters on the hall table and went into the kitchen to start the dinner. Peter wouldn't be

TIME TO LET GO

home until after six, so Iain could deliver his mail later. No doubt he would jump at the excuse to have a chat with his hero.

It was a relief to have someone living next door, Amy thought as she peeled the potatoes. The place had been empty since old Mrs Smith died last

By Sheila Aird

September, and she'd missed the odd sound from through the wall.

Then on the last day of the old year, at a quarter past eight in the morning, a large van had appeared.

Three men began to unload an assortment of furniture on to the pavement just as Amy hurried down her path, intent on catching the early bus to town.

"Good morning."

Amy paused in surprise. A tall, solid, dark-haired man with an attractive smile stood on the pavement, clutching a huge china dog in one arm and a shiny-leaved cheese plant in the other. She guessed he would be about her own age.

"Oh . . . good morning," she said. "You must be —"

"Peter Hamilton, your new neighbour."

"Hello — I'm Amy Townsend. Welcome to Blossomfield Road, Mr Hamilton." She glanced at her watch and smiled. "Look, sorry, can't stop or I'll miss my bus. I'll be back around six. If there's anything.you need just give me a buzz."

"Thanks." His smile widened. "I will."

The picture of the man, the dog and the plant stayed with her all day.

"I've never known anybody to have so many books," Iain said that evening. "I helped him to stack them in the shelves in the alcoves at each side of the fireplace. It took absolutely ages."

Amy was horrified. "You did what?"

"Oh, Mum, don't be such a fusspot. Peter's OK. We had a long chat about bikes."

At seventeen, Iain had a habit of taking people at face value, and as he was bike mad, anyone like-minded would be his best friend.

But now, three weeks later, Amy could agree Peter Hamilton was more than just OK. She'd been charmed by his gentle sense of humour and easy-going manner. In an amazingly short time they'd become good friends.

The chops were almost ready and the vegetables warming in the oven when Amy heard Iain's key in the lock.

"Great! You're early," he said, tossing his anorak across a convenient chair. "I'm starving, and I'm playing badminton in an hour. Did you wash my white shorts?"

Amy followed him into the kitchen.

"Yes, and they're even ironed." She smiled resignedly. "But if I hadn't rescued them from under your bed you'd have had to wear your jeans tonight!"

"Thanks, Mum," he said over his shoulder as he began to wash his hands at the sink. "I suppose I'll have to learn how to do my own washing — and ironing — come September."

"Time enough yet," Amy muttered as she dished up the meal.

It wasn't true. September would be here before they knew it, and Iain would be gone. The house would be empty without him.

Watching him tucking into his meal, she felt an ache at her heart. She was so proud that he'd been offered places at two universities on the strength of his exam results.

If only he'd decided to take up the Glasgow place! Why was he so set on leaving home?

"I'm so proud of you, darling," was all she'd said.

She hadn't asked about the course, or where he intended to live when he went to Aberdeen. Time enough to ask about that later, when he'd passed the next lot of crucial exams.

SHE was wiping the last plate when she remembered Peter's letters. Iain had raced off to the sports centre after gulping down his meal, so she would have to deliver them herself.

"Sorry, I should have brought these earlier," she said, stepping into the hall which was a replica of her own.

"I'd rather you hadn't brought them at all." Peter groaned. "Buff-coloured envelopes always contain bills. Bills have to be paid — eventually."

Suddenly he smiled, and she was reminded of their first meeting. Her eyes moved to the impressive china dog sitting proudly on the hall table. "He's gorgeous," she said without thinking.

Peter followed her gaze.

"Yes, and he doesn't bark," he said, tongue in cheek. "My daughter gave him to me on the day she went off to college in Edinburgh. I was chuffed to bits when she staggered into the house with him. Doesn't seem like eighteen months ago!"

"You must miss her."

He nodded ruefully.

"Life was never dull when Julie was around. She saw the funny side of everything. But at least now I can use the phone any time I like, and listen to Pavarotti instead of pop!"

"It's not the same, though, is it?" Amy said, thinking of Iain.

"No." He paused. "It's funny to think that three years ago life was hectic. Then the boys left — I'll never forget the day they went.

"My wife had died six months before, and there they were, standing on the station platform, looking more like twelve-year-olds than eighteen. I wanted to bundle them into the car and take them home again. But at least they had each other. They're twins."

Amy nodded, imagining two younger versions of Peter Hamilton, facing the world together. No doubt they would break a few hearts.

"I'd better go," she said, and turned.

"Excuse the clutter," Peter said as she bumped into a bag of golf clubs leaning against the wall. "I'm still unpacking boxes, but I can't find room for everything."

"I know the feeling," Amy sympathised. "I had to get rid of masses of stuff when we moved, after —"

She stopped. The words "after Richard died" remained unsaid. The past was locked in her mind, and she had no intention of letting it out.

"Apart from lack of space, are you settling in OK?" she asked.

"Yes, thanks to your son."

Amy frowned.

"I hope he hasn't been bothering you."

"On the contrary, Iain's a mine of information. He's filled me in about everything from where to buy the best steak pies to what's on at the cinema.

"He's so enthusiastic about everything. Honestly, he's great company!"

Obviously he meant it and Amy glowed at his praise.

"I'm dreading September, when he goes to university," she confessed. "Aberdeen seems so far away."

"Nonsense. It's only a few hours on the train. He'll be back every other weekend." He grinned. "If only to get a good feed and to get his laundry done."

He'd touched a nerve.

"I don't want him to come home every other weekend," Amy said bluntly. "I don't want him to go at all."

For a moment silence hung between them.

"He was offered a place at university in Glasgow, you see," she said more evenly.

"And you wish he'd taken it?"

She didn't have to think.

"It would have been much more — convenient."

"Not for Iain."

Amy was too surprised to say anything.

"Look, Amy. I know it's painful but you've got to face it — he's not your wee boy any more. They all have to go sometime."

"But not yet. It's too soon."

"It's his life. Let him go without a fuss, and he'll come back willingly. Mine did." He paused and she looked up at him. "Don't make him feel guilty because he wants to spread his wings a bit."

Amy caught her breath.

"I didn't know he felt guilty. Obviously you know something I don't."

Peter thought before answering.

"I think he wants your approval. Oh, he didn't tell me in so many words, in fact he was quite subtle about it.

"It wasn't until after he'd left the other day that I realised what he was getting at. I assume you've been avoiding the issue."

"Why? What did he say?"

Peter shrugged.

"He asked how I felt when Julie left home. Did I help her to get digs, and did we talk about her course? Things like that."

"And?"

"I told him the truth. I got caught up in Julie's enthusiasm. We shared the experience of finding somewhere for her to stay, then the new friends and the course itself.

"I'm not saying the parting was easy. It was pretty awful. But after she left she phoned every night for several weeks — reversing the charges, of course!" He smiled, remembering. "Looking back, we had a lot of fun. And it brought us closer."

"Perhaps there was no alternative for Julie," Amy said. "Iain has a choice."

Peter's expression changed.

"Iain made his choice months ago," he said quietly. "No matter how upset I felt about my kids leaving home, I wouldn't have stopped them just because I'd be left on my own."

Amy bit back a protest as the words arrowed home.

"You don't understand," she said bleakly.

"Oh, yes, I do," Peter replied.

Faithful Friend

*M**Y faithful pet of many years,
How dear you are to me,
My feline friend with knowing look
Who listens silently
To everything that's going on
With our family,
Who pads about and pricks up ears
With curiosity.*

*You have a certain canny sense,
You always seem to know,
The days when I am out of sorts,
The times I'm feeling low.
Then you come padding up to me,
Just putting on a show,
And wind yourself around my legs
Miaowing as you go.*

*You know just how to make me laugh
And lift my spirits high.
Just gazing at your graceful form
I look at you and sigh.
I ask myself this question,
I ponder how and why,
When did this velvet friend become
The apple of my eye?*
— *Kathleen Gillum.*

B ACK in her own kitchen, Amy was consumed with increasing anger and disappointment. Of course she realised Iain had his own life to lead. Since Richard had been killed in the car crash she'd been careful not to interfere, guiding him rather than laying down the law on many occasions.

But this time it was different. He wouldn't be eighteen until April, for goodness' sake! He was too young to fend for himself.

Then, without warning, her thoughts flew back to her own seventeenth year.

She and Richard had just met. From the beginning there had been no doubt in their minds that they would be married. And they were — three days before her nineteenth birthday. Within eighteen months they had all the responsibilities of a mortgage and a baby.

But they didn't have her mother's blessing.

Without saying a word, her parents had made it clear they thought she was far too young to know her own mind. Although she'd been eager to discuss her plans with them, their disapproval had made it difficult even to broach the subject of marriage.

Still she'd been determined to marry the man of her choice. The wedding had been a small affair — an indication of Mother's feelings towards her only daughter?

Even now, almost twenty years later, she could feel there was still a flaw in their relationship. Did she really want the same thing to happen between herself and Iain?

FERRY TALES

Oban to Craignure (Mull)

by Colin Gibson

Duart (Mull)

The ferry from Oban takes 45 minutes to reach the pier at Craignure in Mull. Buses are there to convey passengers to all parts of the island.

But if you know by experience that life slows down a little in the West Highlands and Islands, you will take time to admire the view across the water to the Isle of Lismore, quite near, to the noble mountains of Appin, more distant, and more distant still, Ben Nevis, rising unmistakably "abune them a'."

Near Craignure, too, is that one-time stronghold of the Lords of the Isles, Duart Castle, the home of the Clan Maclean.

At one time, Duart was no more than a square keep planted on the rocky coast. The walls were 12 feet thick and the only access to friend or foe was by way of a steep stone staircase on the seaward side.

In more recent times, Duart was restored and renovated and visitors given a kindlier welcome.

The resident Macleans are passionately Scottish and have gone far in establishing Duart Castle throughout the world as the spiritual home of the Macleans.

Tears sparkled in her eyes and she stared into space. She was loth to admit it, but Peter was right on two counts.

Iain wasn't her wee boy any more. He was a young man who was perfectly capable of making his own decisions. And she didn't have the right to stop him from leaving just because she would be left on her own. There, she'd admitted it at last.

Tears spilled on to her cheeks, but she didn't attempt to wipe them away. She wept for herself, and the end of another chapter.

She was sitting at the kitchen table drinking a cup of coffee when Iain arrived home.

"Had a good time?" she said casually.

"Yes, but Robbie and I lost."

"Robbie?"

"Robbie Macleod. He starts uni in September, same as me."

"At Aberdeen?"

Iain bit his lip.

"There'll be four of us, Mum. We're hoping to share a flat."

"I didn't realise you'd thought about a flat." Amy tried to sound matter-of-fact. "Maybe it's time we had a talk about this course."

Iain sat down opposite her.

"I'm sorry, Mum. You won't make me change my mind. If I pass the next exams I'm going to Aberdeen. It's what I want to do."

His stubborn frown reminded her of Richard and she smiled.

"I know, love," she said. "And I think you're doing the right thing."

NEXT morning, the path from the front door to the gate was a sheet of ice.

"Hold on to me, Mum," Iain said as she locked up.

"Why? Are you frightened your old mum falls and breaks a leg?"

Iain grinned. "No, I was hoping you'd let me lean on you."

Laughing, she clutched his arm and they slithered towards the pavement.

At the gate, Iain went off in the opposite direction while Amy inched her way towards the bus stop. The cold, sharp air tugged at her breath and gave her senses a boost.

Suddenly she felt a hand on her elbow.

"D'you need a hand?" Peter's voice was low.

Amy looked up at him, and her heart began to pound.

"Yes, please," was all she said.

With his hand firmly supporting her, they walked on.

"I'm sorry about last night," she said.

"Oh." His grip tightened as she slipped on an icy patch. "Careful!"

Amy stopped and turned to look at him.

"Didn't you hear what I said?" Her breath hung like a web in the icy air. "I have to let him go. I know that now."

"I heard you." He smiled at her. "It's not easy, is it?"

"But it's for the best. You'll be pleased to know we had what Iain called a 'heart-to-heart' last night."

"And?"

"Oh, Peter, he's scared to death."

"And excited?"

"He can hardly wait. Everything came pouring out — the exams, the course, his job prospects when he gets his degree — I didn't realise how he felt."

"It's a big step."

"For me too." Suddenly Amy was nervous. "I'll probably weep buckets. Nothing will be the same after he goes."

"You'll cope. We all do." Without taking his eyes from her face, he took her hand and tucked it inside the crook of his arm. "Anyway, I'll be here if you need a shoulder to cry on."

Amy's heart missed a beat, then her spirits took wings.

"Thank you. I'd like that — very much."

They went on their way arm in arm. ■

MISTY'S

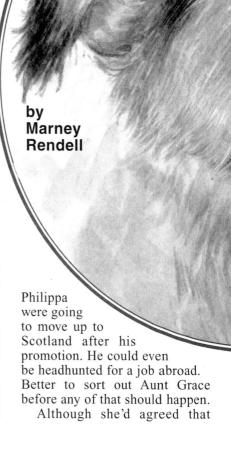

**by
Marney
Rendell**

I'LL never have another," Grace said unsteadily as the door to the surgery closed softly behind her.

"Everyone says that, Mrs Weaver," the veterinary nurse said gently. "Maybe you'll feel differently in a few months . . ."

But Grace knew she would never have another dog. The retirement apartments didn't allow pets — except the ones you already had when you moved in. She'd known about this, of course. Giles had pointed it out when they'd fine-toothcombed the lease.

"It's just as well, Aunt Grace," he'd said. "After Misty's gone, you wouldn't want another pet at your age."

It was strange, Grace had thought, how the older you got, the more people assumed a God-like knowledge of what you would, or wouldn't, want. But she knew he was right. Dogs can live for sixteen years — she'd be nearly ninety then.

It had been Giles who'd told her she was vulnerable, living alone in the Victorian detached house where she and Walter had spent most of their married life. Better to move into a retirement flat, with a resident warden, he'd said. Especially now he and Philippa were going to move up to Scotland after his promotion. He could even be headhunted for a job abroad. Better to sort out Aunt Grace before any of that should happen.

Although she'd agreed that

LEGACY

Walter's greenhouse glinting in the comforting glow of light from the houses beyond the bottom fence.

Then she'd prime the teamaker, lift Misty on to the bed, and they'd be asleep in two shakes of a lamb's tail, as Walter used to say.

The house had sold quite quickly, almost before she'd realised what was happening. Giles disposed of the welsh dresser, the dining table with the six chairs, and other furniture unsuited to a flat. He took the grandfather clock and a couple of oil paintings home — for safe keeping, he said.

Grace wasn't fooled, but didn't mind. He'd get them one day anyway — she'd no-one else to leave things to. And she had some money left over from the sale of the house, in spite of the inflated prices of the retirement flats at Oak Stone Court.

Misty had settled in well.

The only other pets were Dr Benson's Siamese cat and a yellow budgerigar whose cage swung from a stand by Miss Manston's lounge window.

the house and the big garden might become difficult to manage, Grace had never felt at all vulnerable in Greenwood View. Some nights she'd stand at the bedroom window, watching the waving lilac, or the panes of

GRACE stumbled from the vet's surgery, taking no pleasure in the warm spring air.

73

Down the High Street and into the suburban roads Misty had enjoyed padding along. Past the hedge that had held some unknown fascination for the little dog.

Grace stared resolutely ahead. She mustn't break down here — she might see someone she knew.

Once, Mrs Conrad had caught her mopping up a puddle in the lift, one of Misty's mistakes made just before her illness. Mrs Conrad hadn't looked too pleased, so Grace pretended something had leaked from her shopping bag.

She'd half expected a comment from Denise, the resident warden, but had heard nothing.

The days had been filled with Misty's walks and Grace's passion for embroidery. And every Friday, she sneaked her shopping trolley past the lounge where the residents met weekly for afternoon tea, hoping Denise wouldn't see her and invite her in.

She could even hear the jollity as she came down in the lift. It was kind of Denise, of course. But Grace was in the habit of doing her shopping on a Friday. Anyway, she'd always felt shy in large groups. She, Walter and Misty had been sufficient company for each other.

And sometimes, in the long hours, Grace would agonise over whether she could ever adapt to this alien communal life.

* * * *

She turned into Oak Stone Court and pressed the secret buttons that opened the security door. In the cushioned elegance of the residents' lounge, Denise was dismantling a completed jigsaw on the coffee table. A new pile of books indicated the weekly visit from the mobile library.

When she was safely inside the lift, the tears overflowed, sliding down her cheeks unchecked. She struggled for control as the lift stopped gently at the second floor.

"Why, Mrs Weaver, whatever's the matter?" Miss Manston's brown brogues were firmly planted on the landing as the doors parted.

"The vet said there was no hope, no hope at all . . ." Grace hurried down the corridor, in spite of Miss Manston's restraining hand on her shoulder.

"Misty? Oh, my dear — I'm so sorry." The rich tones did sound genuinely sympathetic. "If there's anything I can do . . . ?"

Grace delved for her key, mumbled her gratitude, and retreated behind the sanctuary of the oak front door, praying no-one would call.

She'd never been one to express her emotions in public and now she'd let herself down in front of Miss Manston.

She needed to cope with her loss in the way she knew best — alone.

The news went round like wildfire. Some residents offered sympathy, while others seemed almost to be avoiding her. She understood. It was a matter of not knowing what to say.

She remembered some folk had crossed the road to avoid her after Walter died. Not to be unkind, she was sure. They just didn't realise how much she longed to talk about him.

This time it suited Grace. She preferred to be alone. However hard she tried, she couldn't see the other residents as friends. Anyway, it wouldn't be right to burden them with her grief.

She put Misty's feeding bowls away in the kitchen cupboard. The squeaky toys were left in the dog basket. To move those already would seem a betrayal somehow, as if she were trying to erase the memory. Yet her heart ached with such emptiness whenever she looked at Misty's photo, she hid the silver frame in the sideboard drawer.

M RS WEAVER, I do hope you won't mind my asking . . ." Miss Manston emerged from the residents' lounge as Grace ventured out for a walk a few days later. "My niece has asked me for a long weekend, but I have a little problem — Tufty to be precise."

Grace listened politely, wondering what Miss Manston's budgerigar could possibly have to do with her.

"I've always taken him with me before, but my niece has developed an allergy — absolutely no feathers allowed. I wondered — could you possibly put some seed in his pots and check his water for three or four days?"

Miss Manston had been kind when Grace had first arrived. She was social secretary at Oak Stone Court, and had explained about whist drives and theatre outings. She had also been kind the day Misty had died. It would have been churlish to refuse.

So, the following Sunday, Grace found herself in Miss Manston's lounge, topping up seed pots while Tufty supervised with a critical eye. He flitted about the cage, a splash of yellow in the morning sunlight.

Grace clucked through the bars as he admired himself in the mirror, and was surprised to find she'd spent a whole hour enjoying his antics.

The following day she cleaned the cage, though she hadn't been asked to, and was rewarded with a virtuoso performance on the swing.

She felt quite disappointed when Thursday, and the last of the visits, came. She was happier than she'd been for days.

But she still couldn't bring herself to put away Misty's toys.

Miss Manston had only been back a day when Dr Benson sprained his ankle. Could Grace possibly let Cindy, his cat, out every day and get her in at night for a week or so? He wasn't even up to taking the lift.

He'd felt able to ask Grace, knowing she was a fellow animal lover, unlike some of the others he could mention.

Of course she didn't mind. Not even when she noticed Dr Benson, sprained ankle or no sprained ankle, seemed perfectly capable of

Ardrossan to Arran

by
Colin
Gibson

Goatfell, Arran

The Isle of Arran lies in the outer Firth of Clyde, 14 miles from the Ayrshire coast, but hardly five from the long, narrow peninsula of Kintyre over to the west.

The ferry, operated by Caledonian Macbrayne, takes passengers and vehicles from Ardrossan to Brodick in 55 minutes.

Buses rendezvous with the ferries at Brodick pier and go round the northern and southern parts. It's also possible to hire a car or a bicycle if you are not a foot-slogger.

Few ferry landfalls can compare to Brodick Bay, with its fine sweep of sands and Goatfell (2866 feet) rising so admirably above the little town. Holiday folk get a delightful welcome!

Arran is an island of contrasts. Around the coast it is pleasantly pastoral and benign, with a natural charm. To visit Corrie, for instance, with its whitewashed cottages, flowery gardens and tumbling burn is to fall in love with the place at first sight.

But the interior of Arran is very different --- a wilderness of bare, granite peaks though, I should add, a "wilderness" that is "paradise enow" for strenuous ridge-walkers and rock climbers.

Though it is the highest, Goatfell is not the wildest peak and to follow the well-marked tourist route to the summit is the highlight of many an Arran holiday.

In its original Gaelic, the name means "mountain of the wind." As an Arran man said to me, "The only goats you'll see are the silly ones who climb this very exposed mountain in a T-shirt and a pair of shorts!"

Happily, for non-climbers, Arran's intimidating hinterland is penetrated by three sweet valleys -- Glen Rosa, Glen Iorsa and Glen Sannox --- and these present, quite safely, wonderful vistas of mountain and glen.

sneaking down to sit in the conservatory from time to time.

And Dr Benson didn't seem to mind when Cindy went into Grace's flat for sardines or saucers of milk, and sometimes even spent nights on her bed.

"Grace —" Denise, the warden, emerged from the laundry room one morning. "Mrs Conrad has a problem."

Another problem, thought Grace. Just send for me . . .

"How can I help, Denise?" she heard herself say.

"She's been having dizzy spells. Would you mind going with her to the Townswomen's Guild for a few weeks? She's Secretary, you know, so she really should be there."

I'm either the Good Samaritan of Oak Stone Court, or they think I've nothing better to do, thought Grace.

"Of course," she said. "That's on Friday afternoons, isn't it?"

So, for the next three weeks, Grace listened to talks on growing an indoor herb garden, the art of cake decoration, and crime prevention in the home. Afterwards there was tea and a chat, and it was really quite enjoyable.

When Mrs Conrad suggested she should join, it seemed a good idea — and perhaps she wouldn't mind helping on the "Nearly New" stall at the summer fete?

"Not at all," Grace said. "I might give one or two things myself."

THAT night she pulled the boxes down from the top of the wardrobe and piled them on the duvet.

Cindy the Siamese watched from her vantage point on the dressing-table — apparently Dr Benson's ankle still wasn't up to letting her in and out.

Grace rustled the tissue. In one box nestled the hat she'd worn at Giles' wedding and would most likely never wear again. Under another battered lid, lay a beaded pale green evening dress, the scent of lily of the valley still lingering in its folds.

Grace remembered the stuffy civic dinners, when Walter was a councillor, and how she'd worn that same dress from year to year, hoping no-one would remember.

Then she unfolded his pinstripe suit, the one she hadn't been able to let go, and felt for the cufflinks and tie pin in an inside pocket.

Grace placed them all carefully into the biggest box. They should get a good price for the charity sale at the Townswomen's Guild.

You can't live in the past for ever. Walter would agree, she was sure.

She turned the ring on her little finger — Walter's signet ring she'd had made smaller. That would never go.

In the kitchen, she collected the dog bowls and toys and put them with the box.

Then she took Misty's photo in the silver frame from the sideboard drawer and placed it by the table lamp.

Now she must get on with baking those coconut tarts she'd promised for Denise's birthday party on Saturday.

* * * *

By Saturday night, the residents' lounge was transformed beyond all recognition. Balloons bobbed, flowers abounded and a huge, hand-painted banner proclaiming "HAPPY BIRTHDAY, DENISE — LIFE

BEGINS AT 40" was strung between the Picasso prints.

Denise, blue uniform abandoned, blossomed in a floral swirly skirt and frilly blouse. They'd all put money towards a crystal bowl which Grace, as the newest resident, had been asked to present at a suitable moment.

Everyone had provided something for the buffet, and Dr Benson's stereo thumped out everything from Mantovani to rock and roll.

Grace took round a tray of cheese straws, cheeks rosy from an unaccustomed glass or two of wine.

"How's your niece's allergy, Doris?" She waved the tray under Miss Manston's nose.

"Allergy?" Miss Manston looked puzzled for a moment. "Oh yes — it's better, Grace, thanks. Strange how these things happen, isn't it?"

Very strange, Grace thought, as Dr Benson and Mrs Conrad whirled past doing a Viennese waltz, almost knocking her over.

She watched them career into the conservatory. Dr Benson's sprained ankle had apparently miraculously recovered, and Mrs Conrad's dizzy spells seemed to have disappeared, too.

The evening passed in a contented haze. Grace even found herself putting her name down for the museum excursion and the "Phantom Of The Opera" trip.

It was past midnight when the laughing crowd spilled from the lift and Grace finally reached her front door. The telephone was ringing. It was Giles — almost exploding through the earpiece.

"Aunt Grace — I'm sorry to ring so late — I've been trying to get you all evening."

Grace had barely opened her mouth before Giles burst out: "Brilliant news — the grandfather clock and the oil paintings — you remember, I was looking after them?"

Grace remembered her suspicions all too well as Giles went on.

"Well, 'The Antiques Roadshow' was in town and we took them along. And what do you think?"

She hardly knew what to think as the words tumbled from her nephew.

"Ten thousand at least . . . fifteen possibly . . . you could sell them and treat yourself to a world cruise, Aunt Grace."

"That's wonderful, Giles. But I don't know about a cruise . . . ." She laughed. "I've just found out how much fun you can have exactly where you are, if you're with friends . . . ."

"Well, at least buy some champagne to celebrate. Let your hair down for once," he rushed on.

"I've been doing that all evening," Grace said, smiling with relief and shame in equal measure at her earlier ungenerous thoughts.

"Aunt Grace," his voice became muted. "How are you coping without Misty? Whatever you do, don't grieve too long. Think back to

Weathercock

Perched on the spire
The weathercock sees,
Like a broad green floor,
The tops of trees:

Sees cottages strewn,
Like tumbled toys,
And, like walking dolls,
The girls and boys.

A flock on the hill
Is a patch of white,
Like snow that has drifted
During the night.

On the horizon,
Far as can be,
He sees the bright line
Of the glittering sea...

— Berta Lawrence.

all the times of love and happiness she gave you."

"And the happiness I've found, because of her," Grace said softly. "But I can't explain that at twenty past twelve!"

Strangely wide awake, Grace rooted about in the top cupboard and unearthed the embroidery pictures she'd produced over the years. Twenty-seven — no, thirty of them, just gathering dust. She placed them carefully in the box for the charity sale. They might as well do good for someone, and she could always make some more — if she could possibly find the time! ■

I DO so worry over Sally sometimes." Sheila sighed. "She's such a little tomboy."

"I bet you were as well." Betty had come in from next door, a noble volunteer for the wedding sewing, provided she wasn't given anything more hazardous than bits of hemming where it didn't show.

It was such beautiful material, and so expensive! Her hands were all a-tremble at the mere thought.

Sheila had been deeply grateful for the offer since time was running short. Two days to go and all that catering . . .

"Of course you were a tomboy." Sheila's mother nodded, glancing up from putting tiny beads on to the bridal bodice. "I quite despaired of you at times, and yet you turned into the most bewitching girl. Just ask your husband! After all, you've always been his favourite model."

Sheila blushed becomingly. Dave was an illustrator and often, when his inspiration for heroines ran dry, he'd sit her down and sketch her, even if he had sometimes to change her wavy hair from auburn to a duller shade, and her eyes from vibrant green to blue.

"Oh, Mrs Johns, I can't imagine Sheila as ever being the least unfeminine," Betty said.

"Well, when she had her hair close cropped, and insisted that she'd die before she'd wear a skirt . . . And she didn't care too much for soap . . ."

"But I was very young," Sheila protested. "I grew out of all that nonsense. I took a pride in my appearance later. So much so that you used to chide me I was vain!"

"Your memory's playing tricks on you." Mrs Johns laughed. "Poor Sally's barely twelve, and *you* were definitely going on thirteen before you found out what a mirror was."

"Maybe," Sheila conceded, "but it's different nowadays. Kids mature earlier."

"Stuff and nonsense!" Mrs Johns snorted. "They all mature in their own good time. There's nothing you can do to hurry it."

"Besides," Betty said wistfully, "they're only little for so short a time. There hardly seemed to be a day between my Keith starting kindergarten and his graduating from college.

"As for Martin, I'd almost be prepared to swear it can't be fifteen years ago I had him!"

"Still, I wish Sally would grow up just a bit, for her sister's sake." Sheila frowned. "It's bidding fair to ruin Katy's day, having Sally galumphing down the aisle behind her.

"Did you know she wants to wear Doc Martens underneath her bridesmaid's dress?"

The other two collapsed in

giggles, and for a moment Sheila's face lightened. Then she glanced through the window and grew solemn again.

"Look at her right now! She's up the apple tree and crawling out along a branch towards the fruit. Oh!" Sheila put her hands across her eyes. "I just can't bear to watch."

"I'll call her down," Betty said, rising.

"Please don't! The sudden noise might tip her off balance, and we've quite enough to cope with in the next two days without broken bones and crutches."

"Oh, I wouldn't worry," Mrs Johns remarked, quietly complacent. "If Sally's anything like you — and you were such a terror for the trees — she'll bounce.

"Do you recall the day I made you your first proper party frock?

You dragged it on, completely unimpressed, and couldn't possibly sit still for half an hour while we waited for your lift to come.

by
Olwen
Richards

The Tearaway

"No, out you rushed into the garden with old Tig, the collie, romping round your ankles. Then the pair of you were up the oak and heading for the tree house your dad had built you.

"Always had more love than sense, that man, you know," she added fondly. "Well, there you are, all wobbly, when Tig caught sight of some stray cat and gave a mighty 'Woof', and down you tumbled, straight into a pool of mud.

"I never got that pink crushed velvet clean, but you scrubbed up a treat. Not even bruised! I bet you Sally's just the same."

Betty, hiccuping with laughter, reached for a paper hankie, snagged her finger on a pin and yelped in horror.

"Oh no! Blood! I've got it on the dress!"

"We'll sponge it off," Mrs Johns soothed. "There's no harm done. It's only on the seam allowance . . ."

S HEILA shut her eyes and ran her hand across her forehead wearily. If only she and Dave had had the money to go out and buy everything for their daughter's wedding without all this do-it-yourself. But, of course, his income was unpredictable.

In "fat" years they had done the house up bit by bit and put a little cash away towards the "lean" times. Perhaps they should have been less stubborn about Katy's offer to help towards the cost.

"It's sweet of you and Rob," Sheila had said, "but you're going to need every penny when you set up home."

"We'll manage. Like you and Dad."

But Sheila had been adamant, and so had Dave. Admittedly, they'd "managed". More than twenty years they'd "managed", but they wanted something better for their children. So it had become a home-made wedding.

Dave got a discount through a colleague on the stationery and the photos, and he'd grown the flowers himself. Sheila undertook the sewing and the catering.

The catering! She took a deep breath. The final hurdle . . . half the food was safely in the freezer, but the other half was all last-minute. Tomorrow would be chaos.

Thank goodness Katy wouldn't be arriving till night. With luck, she'd never know the traumas which had gone into this week's preparations. Sheila would be efficiency personified by the time the bride got here — she hoped!

"I only wish I could believe you about Sal, Mum. I've so much on my mind without my little tearaway."

"Well, don't you worry any more. I'll sort her out for you."

Betty, gazing at the sticking plaster on her finger, gave a rueful smile.

"And I'll volunteer to help you with the food, shall I? I'm much,

much safer with a knife than with a needle!"

Mrs Johns tiptoed across the landing, peered down into the hall and saw a line of light beneath the kitchen door. She smiled, and the muffled sound of Sheila's blender drifted up behind her as she tiptoed back to Sally's bedroom.

"Right, then, miss. Your mother's busy with the buffet, so we've got a chance to practise!"

Sally pulled a face.

"Don't want to, Gran."

"Sorry, sweetheart, but for just the next two days, what you want doesn't count."

Sally's face grew thundery.

"I didn't mean it quite like that," Mrs Johns corrected herself. "It *does* count, very much. But what you have to do is learn to want what's best for Katy.

"It's her big day, you know, so doesn't that make sense? You'd hate anybody else to spoil it, wouldn't you?"

"Suppose so." Sally pouted.

"Well, we'll have to set them an example."

Sally nodded, grudgingly. She wasn't used to being considered as a model of behaviour, and unexpected pride caught her off guard.

She didn't even jib at being zipped into the floaty dress. Indeed, she gave a hasty sideways glance into the mirror, and her eyes widened, though she wasn't sure she really liked the stranger staring back at her.

She tossed her tousled head rebelliously against the fast-approaching comb.

"I only want to get the general effect," her gran said soothingly, producing Sally's favourite toffee from her pocket as if she was approaching a wild horse with sugar lumps.

But Sally shied away.

"Not having stupid flowers in," she mumbled through a sticky mouthful of toffee.

"Oh, fair enough. They're not important for the practice, only for the proper ceremony. But I'm afraid you'll simply have to try the walking part.

"It's such a long way up the aisle in church. If we go up and down the landing half a dozen times, now, while Mum's not going to see and interfere . . . ?"

She held her hand out in a gesture of conspiracy Sally found quite irresistible.

There's nothing makes a task less irksome than the hint of doing it behind someone's back, Mrs Johns thought triumphantly, though she was at great pains not to glow with the victory.

"Right. Lift your skirt a fraction, Sal, and take a small step forward. Small, mind you, we're being ladylike."

The skirt was duly hitched, a little awkwardly. Mrs Johns stood back and groaned. The hitched-up skirt revealed an instant problem.

"Oh, not in those! We'll have to find the pumps that you'll be wearing, sweetie. After all, you can't take dainty steps in clumpy boots."

"Can so!" Sally tried to demonstrate.

Three heavy strides and she had reached the stairhead. She turned, preparing to retrace her path along the landing, but the flowing skirt swung softly in between her ankles, tangled in the laces of her boots and tripped her.

Wildly clutching for the banister, she slipped and slithered, bumping to the very bottom of the flight of steps, and landing in a sobbing, frightened heap.

"It's only shock," Mrs Johns said, attempting to conceal her own concern, as Sheila rushed from the kitchen to rock her white-faced daughter in her arms. "No broken bones."

"Oh, Mum!" Sheila raised a reproachful face. "Whatever were you doing?"

"Having a rehearsal, dear. I wanted things to be quite perfect. I should have realised there wasn't space up there, I should have made her take those wretched boots off . . ." Her mother's voice tailed into silence as the tears came.

Sheila swallowed her anger with some difficulty. She didn't need her mother being as irresponsible as her younger daughter. But they'd both been frightened, and a row would serve no purpose at the moment.

"There's no harm done," she murmured, as Sally blew her nose.

"Oh, but there is! My dress is torn," Sally cried, fingering a swathe of damaged silk.

Sheila closed her eyes and prayed for strength before she took a careful look.

"It's just the underskirt," she answered, trying to sound calm. "We'll have it fixed in no time, won't we, Mum?"

But Mrs Johns was trembling too much to hold a needle.

"Thank goodness," breathed an anxious Betty, summoned from next door again, "it's in a place that isn't going to show my sewing up!"

S HEILA sank into a corner of the sofa as music swelled and people danced around her.

Everything had gone superbly. Katy had floated up the aisle, a mother's dream, a father's pride.

There had been tears, of course, but they were far outweighed by smiles and laughter. All the food had disappeared amid appreciative comments. Yes, everything had gone supremely well.

Even Sally's petticoat had mercifully stayed out of sight, and the mended tears were scarcely noticeable even when you knew. Sally had worn her satin pumps without a protest for the ceremony, and had been impeccably polite to all the guests at the reception.

If only, Sheila mused, this could have been the start of graceful womanhood instead of one small blip on the horizon!

Suddenly she was aware of someone's hand on hers, a gentle squeeze, and then a whisper in her ear.

Opening her eyes, she followed her mother's pointing finger.

"Oh!" she murmured happily. "At last!"

"I told you." Her mother beamed. "There was a lady hidden in the tomboy, just waiting to come out. And now she has."

On the floor among folds of outspread silk sat Sally, her wilting posy shyly yet flirtatiously held up against her cheek, gazing enraptured at the handsome friend of Betty's youngest son . . . ■

So Fresh And Fair

I MEANT to turn the bedrooms out,
I meant to brush the stairs,
And dust the crannies, maybe catch
A spider, unawares . . .

So many tasks I had in mind
This morn, in early spring,
But then, the sun shone teasingly;
I heard a blackbird sing.

And when I opened wide the door,
The breeze blew in so sweet,
I almost fancied I could see
Primroses, at my feet . . .

Green bracken fronds, wild cherry-bloom,
Young rabbits at their play,
And treetops stirring, dreamily,
Along the woodland way.

And so beguiling was the spring,
The world so fresh and fair,
That suddenly I longed to go
Out in the sparkling air.

I told myself this lovely day
Will never come again,
So — on with jacket, work will keep . . .
Tomorrow it might rain!

— Kathleen O'Farrell.

PENNY for them?" Anna Dryburgh turned away from the window at the sound of her sister's voice and smiled.

"Oh, I don't know, Liz. I suppose I was just wondering why I ever left this place to go to London."

Her smile broadened as she caught the look on her sister's face. "I know! There's no need to remind me that I couldn't wait to leave when I was younger."

"I wasn't about to. I was thinking about all the advantages now," Liz protested. "You're only feeling a bit down because of breaking up with Ken. You'll have to put him behind you and count your blessings." She shifted the baby in her arms and leant against the door jamb.

"Such as?" Anna asked.

"You have a lovely flat and an interesting job, not to mention a new car that Tom would give his eye-teeth for."

The two young women looked at each other and laughed. Tom, Liz's husband, had enthused about Anna's sporty car with its roll-down roof. As a doctor in a rural practice with a growing family, he drove a sensible 4-wheel drive estate car that could tackle country roads in any weather.

"It's only a company car," Anna said, her gaze wistful as she looked at the infant sleeping in Liz's arms, "and the rest doesn't add up to much."

Ken hadn't wanted them to have children. That was just one of the rows they'd had. Another had been over exactly where their relationship should go next, as he had put it. He'd wanted Anna to give up her flat and move in with him to test their compatibility.

"I don't see what your problem is," he'd reasoned. "If we're going to get married anyway, what does it matter that we give living together a go first? Lots of

A Heart Full Of Hope

couples do it. It's the next logical step."

When she'd resisted, he quickly found someone else who was willing to move in with him — one of the secretaries at the large computer company where Anna worked in marketing and Ken was in sales.

Now she was on her own again, one of the worst aspects was that they still worked together for the same firm, and occasionally had to attend meetings together or pass each other in the corridor. She was looking for another job, but in the

**by
Sarah-Jane
Leydon**

meantime, the harsh reality of being alone in a big, strange city had been brought home to her.

Spending a few days with Liz and Tom and their two children, nine-year-old Amy and baby Ben, was a welcome break from job-hunting. But the visit to her home town in North Wales was also a reminder of what she was missing by living in London.

"You seem so content here with Tom and the children," Anna told her sister when they came in from a stroll before bedtime. "I feel as though I've made a mess of my life."

"Don't be silly. You're young, pretty and intelligent," Liz said kindly. "Time will make things better, I promise you."

The next day Anna helped her sister with the household tasks and made a big birthday cake.

"I love baking but I don't bother now there's only me to eat it," she said as she lifted the hot cake from the oven.

"Well, you won't find that problem while you're here. Amy and Tom would demolish this between them in one evening if I let them." Liz laughed.

THE afternoon passed quickly as they drank tea in Liz's comfortable kitchen, and Anna started to feel the stresses and strains of the past few months slowly easing away. She enjoyed feeding Ben his bottle, and, looking down at the warm bundle in her arms, she thought again how lucky her sister was. Anna's reverie was interrupted a second later when Ben's face started to redden and his tiny fists became balls as he screwed his eyes up and opened his mouth for a loud yell.

"Oh dear, what did I do?" Anna asked as she handed him back to his mother.

"Don't worry, you didn't do anything. He's teething and he's often like this. Tom thinks he's going to be an opera singer," said her sister with a rueful smile. Within minutes she had crooned the baby into a fitful sleep, but her face was anxious as she glanced up at the clock.

"Amy will be out of school in twenty minutes or so, but if I put Ben down I'm worried he'll wake up and start crying again. Would you be a love and pick her up?"

"Of course I will," Anna said, glad to be of use. She liked the walk to the school. It was the same one that she and Liz had attended as children.

Amy's face brightened as she saw her aunt standing outside the gate.

"Can we go back along the beach?" she asked as soon as she reached Anna, grabbing her hand and already dragging her in the direction of the shore.

"Why not?" asked Anna good-humouredly.

It was a balmy afternoon after a weekend of storms, and, as far as the eye could see, the beach was littered with pieces of wood and debris thrown up by the rough seas of the previous few days.

Amy darted about the beach, picking up bits of shell and driftwood for the class nature table and bringing them back for Anna to carry.

"I'm not an aunt, I'm a pack-horse," she grumbled as her niece laughed and swooped on another find.

Loaded down as she was, Anna nearly missed the bottle.

She might have passed it by anyway but the unusual blue colour caught her eye and she bent down to pick it up, thinking Amy might be interested. On closer inspection she saw the top had been corked and there was a note inside. Try as they might they couldn't open the bottle, and the two of them hurried home to open it and read what was inside.

"What does it say? Let me see!" Amy pleaded.

The note had come from a ten-year-old boy, Stephen Woods, who lived in Conway, just along the coast.

"He wants a pen-pal!" Amy breathed, her eyes sparkling, and Anna smiled.

"Don't you think he might have wanted the bottle to go a bit farther, darling?" Liz suggested. "Maybe we should throw it back — you could always add your own note, too," she said hastily as she saw her daughter's stubborn expression.

"We found it and I want a pen-pal!" Amy said, and her mother nodded.

"All right. Why don't you write to him a letter while Aunt Anna and I get supper ready?"

"When will he write back?" Amy asked Anna as they walked home from posting the letter to the sender of the bottle.

"Well, it could take two days for your letter to arrive, and even if he writes back at once it could be another two days, so you shouldn't really expect anything before next week," Anna told her, although privately she wondered if the boy who'd thrown the bottle out to sea would bother writing back at all. She remembered her own anticipation when she pulled the note out and shook her head at the foolishness of her disappointment. Had she really expected the letter to be from a young man as lonely as she was?

THE next few days passed pleasantly as the sisters shopped, walked and pottered round the house together. Sometimes they would both pick Amy up from school and sometimes Anna would go on her own and bring Amy back along the beach. In the evenings they'd share a meal and hear about Tom's day at the surgery and his home visits and they'd tell him what they'd done. Tom was due to have one of his rare Saturdays off and he had promised to take them into Chester to choose a new carpet for the living-room.

On Friday Anna went alone to fetch Amy, and smiled as she saw her niece race along the path towards her.

The letter had come that morning, which meant Amy's pen-pal must have written as soon as her letter had arrived at his house. She watched with amusement and curiosity as Amy ripped open the letter and read it quickly, her face shining.

"He wants me to go to tea tomorrow!" she said.

"Tomorrow? But we're going into Chester tomorrow," Anna reminded her niece.

"Oh please, Auntie Anna!"

"If you're sure you don't mind, Anna," Liz said, her pleasant face creased in a worried frown.

"It's no trouble. Amy wants to go so much, and you don't need me to choose a carpet. We can all do something nice together on Sunday," she suggested, and Liz looked relieved.

"I know a pub where the food's great and there's a play area for kids," Tom said. "We could have lunch there tomorrow and go for a walk afterwards."

With the weekend settled to everyone's satisfaction, Anna and Amy drove to Conway the next day.

The address on Stephen's letter turned out to be a small white cottage overlooking the sea. Amy was unusually subdued with excitement as they went up the path and rang the bell.

"Hello — you must be Amy," said a voice, and Anna had to readjust her line of vision to take in the tall, friendly-looking man who had answered the door.

"Mr Woods? I'm Anna Dryburgh, Amy's aunt."

"Come in," he said. "Stephen's setting the table in the garden. I'm Simon, by the way."

"Outside?" Amy asked in delight, and the two adults met each other's eyes and smiled.

Amy was a little shy at first but she and Stephen were soon trying out his new tree house and their carefree chatter drifted up the garden to the table where the adults were sitting.

"I was worried Stephen would be disappointed his bottle hadn't got very far," Anna said.

"No. He was just delighted he got a response. Besides, when he goes home they can be real pen-pals, and in the meantime he's made a new friend."

"Home?" Anna was puzzled. "Are you on holiday here then?"

"I'm not but Stephen lives in Cardiff. His mum's in hospital having another baby and his dad, that's my brother, can't take time off work so I suggested he came to stay here until things are back to normal at home. I'm a teacher so Stephen's been sitting in on my class."

He paused and looked at her, his blue eyes curious.

"Do you live here?"

"I moved away down to work in London for a few years, but I've

FERRY TALES

Elgol (Skye) to Loch Coruisk

by
Colin
Gibson

Loch Coruisq

The Isle of Skye acts like a magnet, not only on the compass needle, but on those who have visited the Misty Isle. It pulls them back again and again.

And the highlight for many a holidaymaker, especially hill lovers, is the motor-launch trip from Elgol across Loch Scavaig to Loch Coruisk in the very heart of the Coolins.

It starts as a sea-going voyage of four miles from Elgol in the south-western tip of the island, and the serrated skyline and mountain crags are in full view all the way.

A landing is made at the mouth of the "Mad Burn", a riotous torrent that has cut its way through the rampart of rock separating the salty Loch Scavaig from the freshwater Loch Coruisk.

The scene beyond almost beggars description, savage and dramatic grandeur with Coruisk, dark and

deep-set, in a mountain amphitheatre of bare and barren crags.

Sir Walter Scott, John Buchan and many other writers have tried to describe it, while Turner and other artists have attempted to portray it and capture its wild and impressive beauty.

Many of the crags look unscalable, but probably you will have noticed that many of the passengers in the launch are well-equipped with rucksacks, coils of rope, ice-axes and other climbing gear.

The eager excitement on their faces shows their enthusiasm for the climbing challenges that lie ahead.

The rest of us will, in due course, return from Coruisk to Elgol, but we are not likely to forget the "Water Cauldron" with its dark waters and soaring crags.

been considering coming back. I like it around here."

Soon conversation between Anna and Simon was flowing as easily as it was between the two youngsters, and when Simon suggested the four of them went for a walk along the beach Anna agreed.

"What gave Stephen the idea to send a message in a bottle?" she asked as they stopped to watch the children playing at the edge of the sea.

"It was my idea, to be honest," he said finally, his smile a little embarrassed.

"It was a nice idea," she assured him. "In fact it was something I've always wanted to do myself. I was so excited when I found the bottle and realised there was a note inside."

It was her turn to feel embarrassed then, as she realised how she had given herself away, but Simon's smile was warm as he looked back at her.

"Maybe we're the ones who should be keeping in touch," he said lightly.

Anna got to her feet quickly. The last thing she wanted was to get involved with another man after the heartache and confusion of the past year.

"It's getting chilly," she said. "I'd better call Amy."

Amy was quite reluctant to leave her new companion, and she chattered excitedly about Stephen and what they had done as they drove home. Anna listened as well as she could but felt slightly distracted, her thoughts returning again and again to a frank, blue gaze and a kind smile.

"Simon Woods? I went to school with him," Tom said in a pleased voice as Anna and Amy told them about their afternoon. "Fancy that!"

"He's a teacher now," Anna said casually, although she was eager to hear more about him.

"That's right, and he works with youngsters with learning disabilities a couple of evenings a week as well. I've met him through work occasionally," Tom added.

"I'm surprised he's not married," Anna said, busy at the kitchen sink.

"Too busy, probably," said Liz, but Tom grunted.

"Had his fingers burned, I heard. He was engaged to a local girl but she left him for some wealthy chap — the one who owned the Northern Hotel."

So Simon had suffered too, Anna thought, as she went to bed that night.

L IZ was right about time making things better, Anna realised as the weeks passed and work became less unbearable. Nevertheless, when her sister rang and told her in a voice full of suppressed excitement that there was a job going locally for a marketing assistant,

Anna found herself taking down the details.

"Tom drove me round to have a look," her sister told her. "It's a company that installs computer systems in hospitals, so it would be right up your street."

"You realise I'd have to lose my gorgeous car — no more test drives for Tom," Anna joked, although she had already decided to apply.

She felt quite light-hearted leaving London and found an even nicer flat in her home town, one where she could hear the sea whispering on the beach. At weekends she saw her family, and went for long walks by the sea with Amy.

"Do you still write to Stephen?" she asked one day, and felt pleased when she heard that her niece had kept in touch with her pen-friend.

"He might be coming back at half-term," Amy informed her, "and we can go round for tea again to his uncle's."

One Saturday as she was going home from the supermarket, loaded with bags of shopping, Anna heard her name called and looked round to see Simon Woods.

"How lovely to see you again!" he said immediately. "Are you visiting your sister?"

"No, I've moved back here," she told him with a smile.

"And have you found any more bottles?" His eyes were even bluer than she'd remembered.

"No, even though I walk along that stretch of beach nearly every weekend," she replied.

"Yes, I try to get out to the beach every day," he said. "I find a walk by the sea clears the mind — opens it up to all the possibilities of life."

His words struck a chord deep inside her, and she glanced down at the bags around her feet and made a quick decision.

"If you're not doing anything right now, maybe you'd like to join me for a bite to eat at home," she said bravely, steeling herself for his polite excuses.

To her relief he looked delighted.

"I'd like nothing better," he said.

As she stood in the kitchen talking to Simon while she prepared a salad for their lunch, she felt a sense of peace and happiness creep into her heart. A gentle breeze carried the tang of salt through the window and she could hear the sea below.

"I've been thinking about that afternoon you and your niece came to the house," he said as they walked down to the shore after their meal. "In fact, I've often thought about you, Anna. I'd like to see you again." His eyes were questioning.

Behind them the tide had swept the shore of all the clutter and debris of the morning, leaving it as clean and fresh as a new beginning, and Anna smiled at him with a heart full of hope.

"I'd like that too," she said. ■

ISLA pushed the last of the boxes back against the living-room wall, straightened up and sighed. Moving house wasn't exactly what she had planned to be doing on December 20. It had broken Isla's heart to leave their old neighbourhood, but Jim had lost his job suddenly and they'd had no choice. Isla plonked herself down on a box and stared gloomily out of the dirt-streaked window.

Oh, she was dreading Christmas this year. There were only five days until Christmas and she still hadn't bought eight-year-old Susie the doll's house she wanted. If they'd been in their old house, the Christmas tree would have been up by now and sparkling. Friends and neighbours would be popping in and out.

Isla plugged in the kettle and thought about last year's tree, an eight-foot pine which stood proudly in the hallway, dripping tinsel and twinkling joyously. The scent of it alone had been magnificent. She remembered Christmas Day, the mingling aromas of turkey, balsam, and cloves and orange from the mulled wine. She was digging about in a box marked *KITCHEN* for some cups when the doorbell rang.

"Hello? Anyone at home?" came a voice from her tiny hallway.

Isla pushed back a strand of fair hair that had escaped from the scarf knotted in the nape of her neck, and stepped over the boxes and toys which lined the route to the front door.

"Hello! Welcome to the neighbourhood!"

"Thanks. I'm sorry I look such a fright. We've only just arrived, as you can see," Isla said, indicating the toys and boxes with a weary sweep of her arm. She blew out, and more stray curls rose on her forehead then fell back.

"I'm Jackie," the young woman, about her own age, said. "John and I have only been here for a few months ourselves. Don't hesitate to call us if you need anything."

By Diana C. Aspin

AFTER Jackie had left, Isla began the task of unloading all the kitchen boxes. She had made tea but could not find the sugar.

As she searched, she thought about the tired reception she'd given her new neighbour and felt ashamed. It certainly wasn't Jackie's fault that Jim had lost his job — or that the hallway was far too poky to house the smallest of trees.

Even the living-room, she thought, standing in the doorway, wouldn't take a tree the size of the one they were used to. She realised she was really feeling sorry for herself but it wasn't just that . . .

Isla remembered her own childhood Christmases. Her father had died when she was three and her mum had worked hard to raise four small girls on her own. There had been little time for tradition, for the fashioning of precious memories.

Christmas had always been spent at their Uncle Bill and Auntie May's. They had been lovely Christmases, but not the same as if they had been in their own home as one happy family. For this reason, the traditions she and Jim had carved out for their family were more precious to her than pure gold.

Tree-decorating had been a special tradition. During the first week of December they bought the tree, raced home, put on the Christmas music, donned woollen caps and set about decorating. The tradition had originated on Susie's second Christmas when they had rushed in out of the bitter cold and forgotten to take their hats off.

She had a photograph — somewhere — of the three of them that her mum had taken.

All of them were wearing their hats. Plump little Susie was reaching up, tinsel dripping from her fingers, Jim was leaning from the ladder with their giant golden angel in his hands, while Isla was on her hands and knees, lovingly

LIKE ALWAYS...

arranging the brocade skirt for the tree.

Isla could see Jim now in his flat tweed cap, herself in a white, woollen ski bonnet with red pom-poms, and Susie in a red cap with white stripes, all of them decorating the tree to the strains of "Chestnuts roasting by an open fire . . ."

Isla sat down heavily on a box in the corner of the living-room. She gazed longingly into the joyous past and let the tears roll freely into her cup of unsweetened tea. Would Jim find a job? Would she make new friends? Where, oh where, was the sugar when she needed it?

"This isn't like you at all, Isla," Jim said, handing her the bag of sugar and the yellow-flowered bowl. "You're usually so positive about things."

"I know, Jim," she confessed, taking in the piercingly blue eyes she'd once fallen head-over-heels in love with. "It's me. I keep on remembering the tree in the hallway and us, and . . ."

She couldn't go on. There was a lump in her throat the size of a beach ball.

"It'll take time to get used to this house and the new neighbours," Jim comforted her, putting his arm around her shoulders and drawing her close. "Now dry your tears and go and fetch Susie from your mum's. She's dying to see her new room.

"I told her that right after Christmas we'll all go out and choose some wallpaper for it, something with frogs on."

"You're right," Isla said, as she eased her arms into the coat Jim held out. "It'll take time."

When Isla arrived at her mum's, she saw Susie's button nose pressed up against the leaded window. Susie jumped up and down and began to wave.

"Mummy!" she shrieked, as she raced to the door and pulled it open. "Mummy, Daddy called and said he's found a tree. It's Christmas in two days! Where are the hats, Mummy?"

She tugged at Isla's sleeve. "Did you unpack them?"

"I don't know where they are, Susie — in a box somewhere. It's too late to put up a tree, love. We haven't even unpacked."

Susie dropped Isla's sleeve. She pursed her lips. Her dark hair sprang joyously from her forehead in a mass of curls. But her green eyes shone with tears above her freckled nose, and Isla immediately regretted what she had blurted out.

"Oh, Susie," she said, kneeling down beside her daughter and kissing the tip of her nose, "we'll try to find the hats. Pay no attention to me."

"Look what Daddy's got!" Susie shrieked as they squeezed into the narrow hallway and hung their coats on hooks.

Jim was on his hands and knees in the living-room putting the tiniest tree imaginable into a holder. Strains of "Good King Wenceslas" filled the small room. He held his arms out wide as Susie rushed in and folded her into them.

"Look what I found!" he announced, as he yanked his hat over his eyes and pulled a funny face.

"The hats!" she screamed. "Put on your hat, Mummy! Like always!"

Like always, Isla thought sadly. How could this Christmas be like always? Isla gazed down at the small tree.

Jim had bought some silver and gold baubles as tiny as pearls, some gold tinsel, a minute gold angel and a string of multi-coloured fairylights.

Jim patted the floor and then held out Isla's white hat with the red pom-poms.

"It's Christmas," he said softly. "It's Christmas wherever we are, no matter how tiny the tree."

A S Isla knelt by him and pulled on her hat, huge snowflakes began to swirl about in the light from the street lamp outside.

Across the road, Jackie was drawing her curtains. She waved, then shrugged and opened her arms as if to say, "Snow, who'd have believed it!"

Isla smiled and waved back.

"Look, Mummy, I'm the tinsel person!"

Susie held a thread of gold tinsel above the tree and let it float down. It caught upon the angel's wing for a second before coming to rest on one of the lower branches. She repeated the process again and again, as she had done year after year.

After dropping each single strand, she gave her traditional shout. "I'm the tinsel person!"

As Jim plugged in the lights he gave his traditional shout of, "Let there be lights! Merry Christmas!"

"Merry Christmas!" Susie shouted and threw herself unexpectedly into her father's arms.

Isla laughed as they tumbled backwards, clinging to each other, and her heart soared higher than it had ever soared. She watched the snow tumbling outside the window, each flake melting as it hit the warmed pane.

The whole room was warmed by their love for each other. This was exactly, as Susie had so lovingly put it, like always.

How foolish I've been, Isla thought, as she watched the fairylights twinkle brightly and the angel smile down on Jim and Susie. Christmas would be special as long as they were together as a family, loving and laughing as they were right now. Like always . . .■

"TAKE two a day, Mrs Durrell," Dr McCulloch said. "One in the morning when you get up and another last thing at night. I'm sure they'll do the trick. Come and see me again in a fortnight."

It had all started the week after her fiftieth birthday party. What a wonderful day it had been. Her daughter, Wendy, and son-in-law, Clem, had done her proud. They'd come laden with parcels and then taken her out for a surprise lunch at an exclusive hotel.

Later, the two grandchildren had presented her with the fruits of their labours. A tapestry of a jungle scene from Sandie, showing a different animal for each of

98

her seven years. It had taken her three months to finish, doing a small square at a time whenever she came home from school. Anne Durrell was very touched by her granddaughter's gift.

And from Cameron, aged eight, a wooden box made during craft lessons in which, he solemnly informed her, she could keep all her jewellery. She smiled at the skew-whiff hinges, the ill-fitting lid and the gouge on the side where the chisel had slipped. What possible better present could a gran have?

She had gone to bed feeling younger than ever and on top of the world. The next day, the feelings of anxiety had started, the loss of appetite, the sinking sensation in the pit of the stomach and that night had been

A Challenge For Gran

by David Bryant

the first of many sleepless tossings and turnings until the dawn thankfully broke.

"You'd better go and see Doctor McCulloch, Mum," Wendy had suggested. "Ask her to give you the once-over. She's very understanding. Everyone says so."

"Just a touch of depression, Mrs Durrell," Dr McCulloch had advised. "It's quite common, especially at your age. For some reason, people feel that fifty is a turning point, a sign of growing old. It's absolute nonsense, of course. Life starts at fifty.

"In fact, I know some eighty-year-olds who are still as sprightly as spring chickens!"

With that, Dr McCulloch had handed over the prescription for the pills . . .

Anne tried hard to hide it from her daughter and her husband. She didn't want to spoil the family excitement. They were all off to Spain for a fortnight. Self-catering on the Costa del Sol.

Not that the grandchildren minded. They would have been just as happy pottering around on the sands at Clacton, building castles and braving the cold waves.

But Wendy and Clem were over the moon at the thought of a foreign paradise. They had been saving up for months and it was to be their first-ever trip abroad.

The bombshell came just before their departure date. Anne had suffered a particularly bad night. Sleepless, fretful and full of worry over the silliest of things. She knew it was irrational but she could not help it.

She forced herself to pour out a bowl of cereal and sat down looking at it unenthusiastically. She felt a ridiculous desire to cry. Then the phone rang.

It was Wendy and she sounded close to tears herself.

MUM, it's me. Bad news, I'm afraid. We're going to have to cancel. Sandie and Cameron have got chicken-pox. They've got spots all over and —" Anne heard what sounded suspiciously like a sniff "—the school doctor says there's no way they can go."

Anne forgot her cereal, forgot everything except the surge of disappointment Wendy and Clem must be feeling. She didn't give a thought to what she was saying.

"Of course you must go, dear. Sandie and Cameron can come to me. Don't cancel, whatever you do."

"But Mum, you know you haven't been well since your birthday," Wendy protested. "And it's a whole fortnight. You can't possible manage."

"Manage? Of course I'll manage, Wendy. Don't forget, I brought up you and your brother, Rob, single-handed. And I hadn't half the experience I have now. A mere chit in my twenties and I coped. You bring them round as soon as you're ready, dear."

Wendy pondered. What her mother said was quite true. She had lost her husband when she was only a young woman— an accident on a North Sea oil rig — and she had battled her way through. But she hadn't been suffering from depression then.

"I don't know what to say, Mum," Wendy said hesitantly. "The flight leaves at six o'clock this evening. It doesn't give you any time to get ready."

"Never mind what to say, Wendy. Get their things together and drop them off on the way to the airport. I'll be ready." And that was that.

FOUR hours later, two very spotty and rather fretful children were unloaded outside Whitebarns House and tucked into bed by their mother and grandmother. Two large suitcases containing their "things" were dumped on the bedroom floor.

There were kisses and waves all round, a few parting tears from Sandie, (Cameron, being too big to cry openly, hid his a bit later in the pillow-case) and then Wendy and Clem drove off, leaving Gran in charge.

She cheered the children up by tipping out the contents of the suitcases into an immense pile on their two beds. Dressing-gowns, underpants, toys, dolls, packets of fruit drops, everything erupted from the bags in an unholy muddle.

The children were demanding. Everything had to be just so.

"Ned likes to be near the window, Gran, where he can see out," said Cameron. "You've got him too near the radiator. He'll get too hot." (Ned was an extremely threadbare giraffe, with one leg, and a wad of stuffing protruding from behind his left ear).

Then Sandie chimed in, "Cameron's trying to hide my liquorice, Gran. Look, he's got it under his pillow."

"That's right, tell Gran everything," Cameron said. "Trust girls to be wet."

"Now that's enough, children," Anne said firmly. "You two are supposed to be taking things quietly according to the doctor."

She was amazed at the energy that children found. Even when they were sick! If she had only a quarter of their go, she would have been content!

Supper was easier than she had expected. A plate of tomato soup for Sandie and a cup of drinking chocolate with toast for Cameron. Clearly the chicken-pox had affected their normally healthy appetites.

She tucked them in, said a goodnight prayer for Wendy and Clem with the children and looked forward to a quiet hour in the armchair before going to bed.

It wasn't to be! She had not reckoned on the itching.

"Can you come, Gran?" The children were scratching ferociously at their legs, chests and arms.

"Children, you must try not to scratch. It'll just make it worse." Anne disappeared into the bathroom and came back carrying a large jar of calamine lotion.

PLOCKTON, HIGHLAND: J CAMPBELL KERR

"Now," she said. "We'll try some of this. It usually works wonders. Slip your pyjamas off, Sandie. And you, Cameron."

She anointed the angels from top to bottom with the soothing lotion and, thank goodness, it did the trick. Twenty minutes later, when Anne went up to check, Sandie was lying on her back, dark hair scattered enchantingly over the pillow.

Cameron was hanging half out of bed, a spaceship dangling from one arm. Deftly she removed the toy and covered him with the duvet. She kissed them both and retired to her own room utterly exhausted and not a little pleased with herself.

Anne climbed into bed, read a magazine for ten minutes and then, drowsily, opened her eyes.

"The pills," she muttered. "Must take one . . . last thing at night, Doctor McCulloch said."

Before she could summon the energy to fetch the bottle from the kitchen, she had fallen into a deep sleep. She did not wake until faint squeals from the children's bedroom told her that it was morning.

The next day passed in a whirl of preparing light meals of mashed potatoes and scrambled eggs, washing pyjamas, changing sheets stained with spilt hot chocolate and topping up the calamine lotion.

The doctor called in and pronounced herself satisfied with their progress. A phone call came from Spain from two anxious parents, but Anne soon stilled their worries and was delighted to hear that they were basking in hot sunshine and enjoying the delights of a crystal-clear swimming pool while the thermometer hovered around the ninety mark.

That night, she again took the pill bottle in her hand and lay back in the warm bed. She was gloriously tired and she couldn't be bothered to pad along to the bathroom for a glass of water to swallow them with. Soon she slept . . .

B Y the end of the first week, the children had taken a definite turn for the better. They started getting up and, with that, Anne's

---

◀ *p.103* ## *PLOCKTON, HIGHLAND*

A HAVEN *for yachtsmen, that's Plockton, on the southern shore of Loch Carron in Highland region.*
And it's a paradise for gardeners, too, thanks to the warming waters of the Gulf Stream. All manner of plants and flowers associated with more southerly climes flourish and bloom in profusion, making the entire area a veritable jewel of the North.

programme changed. Things were getting back to normal.

"Gran, will you help me with this moon-rocket?" She learnt to be nimble-fingered with fiddly little toys and joined in on missions to Mars and beyond.

"Will you play a game with me, Gran?" Draughts, I-spy, Snap, table-football — you name it, she played it. Some she knew from old, others she learnt and, much to her astonishment, found herself roundly enjoying them. She was, she discovered, still a child at heart!

The children's recovery was in no doubt by the time nightfall had come. First Anne had to traipse upstairs to sort out the small problem of a pillow fight. Judging by the thumps and screams and appalling thuds raining down through the sitting-room ceiling, the chicken-pox germs had taken fright and were disappearing fast.

All was at last peaceful and quiet for the night. Or so Anne hoped. Then came the incident of "The Ghost."

"Gran. There's something creepy." Sandie's voice came trembling down the staircase.

Up she went. A volley of information greeted her.

"It was wearing a hood, Gran."

"It keeps going into the cupboard when you switch off the lights."

"It's got horrible red eyes."

"It sort of dances round the room."

Anne went on instant ghost patrol. Every cupboard was inspected, the underside of the bed was peered at and the window catches checked so witches couldn't get in. The "ghost" was the reflection of a hanging dressing-gown behind the bedroom door, seen in the mirror by the dim light of the hall!

This time, as she collapsed into bed, the thought of the pills didn't even enter Anne's mind! And, as for the anxieties and the tearfulness, well, there wasn't even time to gulp back a cup of tea, let alone be depressed.

THE big test, however, was to take place on the day before Wendy and Clem flew back from holiday. The doctor had given the go-ahead and the children were fighting fit. Anne had left this ordeal to the last, because it was the one thing still worrying her. Driving the car.

Before her fiftieth birthday she had whizzed off in all directions. From country lanes to motorways, she'd taken them all in her stride with never a second thought. Then, with the depression, had come a nervousness of driving.

But she had promised the children and there was to be no turning back. A day at the seaside!

She packed the boot with every conceivable requirement. Crisps, lemonade, sandwiches, coffee, biscuits and chocolate cake. A beach ball, a kite, a folding chair, plasters, buckets and spades, overcoats and

Remembered Splendour

HAUNTED by terraced hills
That brush the sky,
Crags where the grey cloud spills
And eagles fly,
Longing the spirit fills
For days gone by.

several changes of clothing followed in their wake. Then they were away.

There was such an avalanche of questions that Anne quite forgot to be worried on the notoriously busy stretch of the main road leading to the coast.

"Are we there, Gran?"

Here, where a hill loch gleams
Through summer haze,
Nothing is what it seems
On stormy days –
Ancient and full of dreams,
These mountain ways!

Those who would beauty find,
Or sweet release,
Treasure within the mind
This mountain peace –
Songs of the trackless wind
That never cease!
                    —Brenda G. Macrow.

"How much farther is it?"

"Can we see a Punch and Judy?"

"Will the tide be in?"

"Can we swim?"

"Do they do donkey rides?"

Anne's head was spinning as fast as the wheels by the time they arrived. But who cared? The children were having a fabulous time.

The last treat had not been intended. It started with that familiar old problem. "I need the toilet, Gran."

As ever, there were no public lavatories in sight, not even a patch of dense bushes. There was only the Grand Hotel, frighteningly expensive and patrolled by a liveried footman in purple trousers and jacket, wearing a formidable moustache and a fierce glare.

It was not remotely suitable. But there was no choice. In they went through the swing door and up to the gilt, opulent reception desk. The request sounded too blunt, too indelicate. Her nerve failed at the last moment. She turned to the children.

"Would you like strawberry teas and cream cakes?"

The price was discreetly printed on the board above the receptionist's head — £5.99 per person. It would make a huge hole in her pension, but children were only young once.

The offer was taken up enthusiastically with a deafening chorus of approval which brought a twitch to the mouth of the undermanager.

"Three cream teas," Anne said firmly. "And, please, where are the cloakrooms?"

THEY all met the incoming flight from Gatwick and it was a happy and hilarious family reunion.

"Mum, you are looking marvellous." Wendy could hardly believe that the wan-faced, tense-looking woman that she had left behind was the twinkle-eyed, blooming, pink-cheeked mother standing in front of her. She stared in amazement. "How's it all gone, Mum?"

"Wonderful, Wendy. We've had a great time and I'm pleased to say that Cameron and Sandie are fully recovered. The doctor doesn't want to see them again."

"Thanks ever so much, Anne." Clem took his mother-in-law's arm affectionately. "Has it seemed a long time?"

"Long, Clem? It's gone in a flash. We've been . . ."

But the words were taken out of her mouth. The children leaping around in wild excitement, tugging at their parents' clothes, were already giving them a blow-by-blow account of the ghost, the space rocket, the doll's tea-party, the pillow-fight, Gran's delicious cooking, the hour-and-a-half of story-telling at bedtime, ("Much better than you do, Mum,") and the day at the seaside and the scrumptious tea at the Grand Hotel.

Clem and Wendy had enjoyed a marvellous holiday, but it was still great to come home to the cuddles and kisses of the children. And they were thrilled to bits at the change in Anne. They could hardly credit how well she was looking.

Nor could Dr McCulloch the next morning when Mrs Durrell came in for her appointment.

by
Colin
Gibson

The Old Man of Hoy

It is the weather-clerk of the turbulent Pentland Firth who controls the timetable for the ferry crossing between Scrabster in Caithness and Stromness in Orkney.

The ferry may well take twice as long in stormy weather than on a day when conditions are reasonably tranquil.

The harbour and pier at Scrabster lie in a sheltered bay west of Thurso. It's a busy port --- fishing boats unloading catches and replenishing stores, yachts and colourful pleasure craft and coasters carrying a variety of cargoes.

The sea-angling is excellent and, for landlubbers, the views across Scrabster Bay to Thurso, Dunnet Head and the ramparts of Hoy are very fine. There is also some remarkable cliff scenery around Holborn Head.

On the north side of the Pentland Firth, Stromness has an equally good harbour, and the little town is quite fascinating with its narrow, paved streets and quaint closes.

A famous inhabitant of these parts is the Old Man of Hoy. He can be seen standing on sentinel duty both by land and by sea.

"Sit down, Mrs Durrell." She took a long look at her. "You're looking much better," she said. "The tablets have done you a world of good."

Anne fished in the pocket of her jacket and triumphantly banged down the unopened bottle on Dr McCulloch's desk.

"There, Doctor," she said. "I won't be needing these, so I'll let you have them back."

Dr McCulloch stared in blank amazement. "You mean . . . you haven't taken them . . . and you're not feeling depressed?"

Anne smiled, a cheerful, bright smile at her GP. "The best cure for depression, Doctor, is to look after two very spotty, chicken-poxy, noisy, demanding, tireless grandchildren for two weeks on your own. Believe me, it works wonders."

For the first time in her career, Dr McCulloch, sitting in her surgery, was at a loss. She just didn't know what to write in Mrs Durrell's medical notes . . . ∎

MY heart sank as soon as I set eyes on her. She was standing, bags at her feet, arms folded tightly across her chest, and a scowl fixed on her face.

My mouth went dry as I approached across the airport waiting area. I could see the badge she was wearing more clearly now — there was no mistake, it read "Katy Walker".

"Katy . . . . ?" I asked nervously.

She turned to stare at me defensively.

I knew Katy was only fifteen and was surprised to find she was quite a bit taller than me. She must take after her father then — Jeff was over six feet. I could also see him in her dark, angry eyes

AIRPORT DEPA

WELCOME

and the way her hair fell into waves.

"Who are you?" she demanded in a strong Australian accent.

"I'm Sarah," I told her quietly.

I'd already decided we should be on first name terms, but it didn't look as though that would make us instant friends.

"Where's my dad?"

"He's in hospital," I explained. "There's nothing to worry about, though," I added quickly. "He's had his appendix out and won't be allowed home for a few days. He was very upset about not being here to meet you."

She shrugged, as if she couldn't have cared less.

I'd had visions of meeting a frightened, shy little girl at the airport, still grieving over the loss of her mother. This hostility took me aback.

Katy was Jeff's only child from his first marriage. He'd been heartbroken when his ex-wife had re-married and gone to live in Australia, taking Katy with her.

Tragically, Fiona had recently been killed in a boating accident and Katy's stepfather had been unable to accept the responsibility of a teenage daughter.

He had enough to do with two-year-old twins to take care of, he'd said in an emotional telephone conversation with Jeff, without the added trouble of Katy.

She was, he insisted, a difficult child — but he didn't explain further . . .

SO poor Katy had not only lost her mother, she'd also been rejected by the man who'd been her father for the past seven years. She'd been forced to say goodbye to her two little half-brothers and then embark on an exhausting journey to the other side of the world.

No wonder the poor girl was looking so upset.

by
**Teresa
Ashby**

TO THE FAMILY"

But there had been no other choice. Katy was too young to stay in Australia alone, and Jeff loved her and wanted her to become part of his new family.

The only reason he'd agreed to her going to Australia in the first place was because he'd thought she would be happier with her mother and new stepfather — they'd be more of a family.

Of course, that was before he'd met and married me. Now we had our own small family — two lovely sons. Michael was five and Joseph, three. I'd left them with a neighbour today, not wanting to subject them to the long drive to Heathrow.

"How was the journey?" I asked lightly.

"All right." She shrugged and started to pick up her bags.

"I'll take some of those," I immediately offered and was taken aback by her sharp response.

"I can manage! I've managed to get this far without any help."

"Well, you don't have to struggle any longer," I said firmly and grabbed the biggest of her bags. "You want a drink or anything before we leave? It'll take about two hours to drive home."

"No."

"Are you sure? Have you had anything to eat?"

"I said no," she repeated angrily. "Now, please, can we just go?"

I felt stung and hurried off, leading the way to the carpark.

It was hard to believe that this was the child I'd been sending cards and presents to for the past six years! That unknown little stranger who meant so much to the man I loved, yet whom I'd never met.

I'd imagined a child, not this aggressive young woman.

The drive home was uncomfortable. Katy rebuffed all my attempts to chat and I was glad when we finally reached the house.

"This is it," I said, pulling up in the drive.

She got out of the car and walked slowly to the front door. I unlocked it and stepped back so she could go in first.

"I suppose it's very different from your home in Australia," I remarked.

When she looked at me, I saw tears shimmering in her eyes.

I wished with all my heart that Jeff was here. He could have reached out to her, hugged her, comforted her.

When I moved towards her, she flinched away.

"Look, I'll show you your room. You can have a bath and put some fresh clothes on while I get you something to eat. You must be starving."

I took her upstairs and opened the door to her bedroom. Jeff and I were about halfway through redecorating it when he fell ill and I'd finished it on my own. We'd done it in fairly neutral shades, knowing she'd probably smother the walls in posters anyway.

"If you don't like it, we can decorate it again. We could tackle it together," I offered quickly, but immediately regretted my impulsiveness..

"It's fine," she said quietly.

"It's your room, Katy," I went on. "I want you to feel at home here."

Back downstairs, I called my neighbour and asked if she could keep the boys for a while longer. When Katy finally came down, I'd made a salad, and to my surprise, she cleared her plate.

"Did you have enough?"

"Yes, thank you," she said, coolly polite.

"Would you like to come across the road with me to collect Michael and Joseph?"

She shook her head.

The boys were curious and eager to meet their new sister, but their meeting was a bit of a disappointment.

They all said hello, eyed each other up and down, then the boys raced off to watch television, while Katy went to her room with a paperback book.

I felt close to tears. I'd been stupid to expect to hit it off with Katy right away — and she was still grieving for her mother, I mustn't forget that. She must be hurting so much inside. I just wished there was some way of reaching her.

Maybe when I took her to see Jeff at the hospital, she'd relax a little. I had this romantic image in my mind of Katy setting eyes on her father, and everything falling neatly into place . . .

M Y understanding neighbour baby-sat again that evening and I drove Katy to the hospital. But Jeff was looking no better, in fact, he looked worse than he had the day before.

Katy stood at the end of the bed and looked at him uncertainly.

"Hello, love." He held out his arms, but she stayed where she was, her face a little flushed.

His hands dropped on to the bed. "I'm sorry about all this," he went on. "I could have picked a better time to get appendicitis."

She nearly smiled.

"You look so grown-up," he said, tears in his eyes. "I always knew you'd be a stunner."

He closed his eyes then and I realised he was in pain, not just overcome by emotion.

"Have you told the nurse you're not feeling well?" I asked anxiously.

He shook his head.

"I want to come home tomorrow. If they think I'm not one hundred per cent., they'll keep me in."

I glanced at Katy. She looked anxious.

"I'm going to have a word with Sister," I said, and hurried off.

Loch Lomond

by Colin Gibson

Loch Lomond has long been famous and never more so than today with its locally-set TV soap and all the rest.

But, at one time, ferrying across the loch wasn't so easy, and the methods of calling the ferryman were rather primitive.

At Tarbet, the general idea was to light a fire on the bank of the loch, and pile on the heather and twigs until a column of smoke was raised and seen across the mile and a quarter stretch of water intervening. In dry weather, this was easy but, on wet days, it was not.

Another way of rousing the ferryman who lived on the Inversnaid side was to give a blast on an old coach horn set there for the purpose, and to continue sending wild blasts over the loch until the boat was seen to be coming.

In his poem, "Highland Girl", Wordsworth mentions her "cabin small, the lake, the bay, the waterfall". But the cabin small was later to be replaced by a fine hotel, incidentally furnishing Dr Johnson's item in his estimate of a beautiful view.

However, whether cabin or hotel, Inversnaid and its waterfall make one of the most charming features along the banks and braes of Loch Lomond's eastern shores. A rich reward for any sightseer.

By the time we left the hospital, we knew that Jeff had a chest infection and wouldn't be allowed to leave hospital for some time.

"He's doing it to be awkward," I joked as we drove home. "He knows it's the only way he'll get lots of chocolates!"

"He still likes chocolate then," she whispered. "I always used to give him a big bar of chocolate on Father's Day."

"He does love you, you know, Katy. He really does. I don't think a day has ever passed when he hasn't mentioned your name."

"Then why did he let my mother take me away?" she burst out.

"He really had no choice," I told her gently. "He might have been able to stop her leaving the country with you, but would you have thanked him now?"

"He should have made her stay," she said. "They should never have got divorced."

"Oh, Katy." I sighed. There was just no answer to that.

ONCE he was taking antibiotics, Jeff began to get better very quickly. I was sure a lot of it was down to his determination to get well. He was looking forward to being at home with Katy.

She started school almost immediately and was swamped with girls, eager to know more about Australia. I suppose we had the TV soaps to thank for all their interest.

The night before Jeff was due to come home, I went to visit him alone.

"Where's Katy?" he immediately wondered.

"Don't worry. She's gone to the pictures with some girls from school." I smiled. "It'll do her good to get out and mix with people her own age."

"I'm glad you're alone," he said. "I wanted to talk to you about her."

"Is she all right? She seems so quiet . . . so unhappy. You are getting along all right, aren't you?"

"She's bound to be unhappy," I said evasively. "She's lost her mother, her family and her home. You can't expect her to be happy about it."

"But I'm her father!"

"You're a stranger to her. She was a little girl when you last saw her. You've got to build a relationship all over again, starting from scratch. It's not easy, Jeff. She's very polite and quiet, but she's not friendly. I just don't know what I can do to get through to her."

"You're not sorry she's come to live with us, are you?" he said quietly, his eyes searching my face.

I managed a smile.

"Of course not. It's early days yet, Jeff. Give her time."

I wished I felt as confident as I sounded.

Instead of getting closer, we seemed to be moving further apart.

The boys had thought it would be great to have a big sister, but soon realised she wasn't any fun.

"She's mean," Michael said crossly one day when she'd told him to get out of her room. "She hates us. I only wanted to show her my reading book."

"She's not mean," I said. "She's very sad."

ON the day I was due to collect Jeff from the hospital, two things happened.

First, Michael woke up with a tummy ache and a slight temperature, so I couldn't send him to school. Then my neighbour called to say her husband was home with 'flu and she daren't have the boys for me.

I put the phone down and bit my lip. It wouldn't be fair to make Michael come all the way to the hospital when he was feeling ill — but I couldn't leave him home alone.

"What's wrong?" Katy looked up from her magazine. I think it was the first time she'd ever started a conversation.

I told her what had happened and she shrugged.

"No problem. I'll stay here with them — if you trust me."

"Of course I trust you, but you've got school."

"I've only got games and art this morning." She shrugged again.

"Are you sure?"

"I wouldn't have offered if I didn't mean it," she said. She didn't sound exactly enthusiastic, but it was the first time she'd ever volunteered to do anything.

"I'll call the school and let them know you won't be in." I smiled, relieved and worried all at the same time.

The postman came before I left for the hospital and brought a letter from Australia for Katy. She looked at it, her face darkened, then she put it to one side.

"Aren't you going to open it?" I asked curiously.

"Later," she answered shortly.

"Is it from your . . . stepfather?"

"I doubt it," she said. "He rarely spoke to me when I was living with him, so I can't see him taking the trouble to write to me."

She sounded so bitter, so full of hurt.

"Oh, Katy," I said, longing to reach out and hug her.

"It's true." She spoke matter-of-factly. "He tolerated me for my mother's sake, just as you tolerate me for my father's sake. We never got on."

I had no time to argue.

* * * *

Jeff was looking a lot better when I arrived at the hospital. The colour was finally back in his cheeks.

With a warning from Sister to take things easy, we set off for home.

I explained to Jeff about Michael being unwell and Katy staying at home to look after him.

"Is that a good idea?" he said anxiously. "I mean, from what you've said, she's not all that happy with the situation."

"I had no choice. Anyway, it seemed important to trust her."

I'd seen very little of Katy really, since she'd arrived. She either went out at night or stayed in her room. When I'd asked if she wanted to come shopping with us, she'd turned me down flat.

"I've a lot of catching up to do with school work," she'd said.

While I'd applauded her sensible attitude, I'd felt a tiny stab of rejection.

It was the same on Sunday when I asked if she'd like to come to church with us. She looked at me as if I was mad even to suggest it.

Maybe I'd been trying too hard . . . Maybe I wasn't trying hard enough . . .

I just didn't know what to do. Was she the type of girl who needed to be pushed, or should I leave her alone to come round in her own time? I felt completely trapped in the situation.

By doing the wrong thing, was I causing irreparable damage to our relationship? And did she really feel as though she were simply being tolerated?

Poor girl. No wonder she was mad at the world.

JEFF looked in through the living-room window before I had the chance to open the door.

"Come here . . . Sssh, look at this."

I stood beside him and looked in. There, on the living-room floor, lay Katy reading aloud from a book while Joseph sat on her back, pretending she was a horse.

"I thought you said she didn't get on with the boys." Jeff grinned.

I stared. I could hardly believe that this was the same girl. She was always so aloof with the boys, not wanting anything to do with them, yet she seemed to be enjoying playing with Joseph now.

By the time we'd opened the front door and let ourselves in, Katy was sitting in an armchair staring into space. Joseph was left kneeling on the floor, looking puzzled.

"Caught you!" Jeff laughed.

Joseph let out a squeal and ran to him, but had to be content with a bear hug. Jeff wasn't allowed to lift anything for some time.

I looked around. She must have moved with lightning speed to have got off the floor and into a chair.

"Hi, Katy," he said. "How are you?"

"All right." She stood up, grabbed her schoolbag and added, "I'll get off to school now. Out of your way."

"No," I said. "You can go back after lunch. Stay, Katy."

She sat down again sulkily.

"How's Mike?"

"Sleeping," she said. "He's not very well, though. I think you should call a doctor. I reckon he's got tonsillitis."

"Oh? How do you know?"

"I've had it myself," she said. "He's got a sore throat, aches all over and he's very hot."

"Right, well I'll call Doctor Madison straight away," I said, going to the phone.

Katy looked at me in surprise.

"Aren't you going to see for yourself first?" she asked.

"Your word is good enough. You're not daft, Katy."

As it turned out, Katy's instincts were absolutely right. The doctor confirmed that Michael did have tonsillitis.

WHAT'S this?" Jeff was sitting in his armchair and had retrieved a screwed-up airmail letter from the bin.

"It came for Katy this morning," I told him. "Hasn't she opened it?"

"Yes." He was busy flattening out the paper so he could read it.

"Hey, you shouldn't . . ."

"It's from Fiona's husband," he said. "He must have written it soon after Katy left Australia."

"What does it say?" I asked, forgetting about being all moralistic about reading other people's mail.

"'I hope you had a good flight', blah, blah," Jeff spoke quickly, his eyes scanning the page. "Aww, listen. 'As we agreed before you left, it would be better to sever all connections now. I'm going to start a new life with the boys . . .' How cruel!"

"But they're her half-brothers!" I cried. "Her only connection with her mother!"

"Now you know," Katy said bitterly from the doorway. "I bet you wish I'd never come here, don't you? I'm nothing but trouble. I wasn't allowed to play with my brothers. He was always afraid I'd hurt them. He said I was big and clumsy and . . . and . . ."

SUDDENLY, the tears began to flow. Jeff and I both ran to her side as her shoulders heaved with sobs.

"I wouldn't have hurt them." She wept. "I love them. He said I'd be jealous of them, but I wasn't, I really wasn't."

This time, I did put my arms around her. If ever a girl needed a hug, Katy did — and badly.

"I know," I said softly and to my amazement, she turned her face towards me and bent so she could rest her head on my shoulder.

"Was he cruel to you?" Jeff asked, his face tight. "Did he ever hurt you?"

"No." She shook her head. "He was all right until the twins were born, then he changed.

"I think he didn't want me any more. If Mum ever tried to make it up to me, he got angry and said she was showing favouritism."

She'd been through so much, this girl, I suddenly realised. It would take us a long time to make her feel loved and trusted again. But we had plenty of time . . .

Michael sauntered in then. The penicillin the doctor had given him had already started to take effect.

"Why's Katy crying?" he asked, staring at her. "Is she still sad?"

"Don't cry, Katy," Joseph said, handing her a tissue.

She looked at each of us in turn and the ghost of a smile crossed her face.

"Come here," Jeff said, holding out his arms. But she looked at me, before she moved, as if for approval, waiting for my smile and nod before going to him.

She'd been deprived of love and the right to give her love — and she had so much to give.

She's upstairs now, reading the boys yet another bedtime story. I can hear them all laughing. The three of them sit squashed in the bottom bunk, huddled around a book.

"Listen to that noise!" Jeff flinches as they squeal and laugh. "I can hardly hear the telly!"

"It's a good noise though, isn't it?" I say happily.

So much has changed over the past few months.

Today, when Katy and I went on a shopping jaunt together (just the two of us, no males allowed), Katy linked her arm through mine. I felt like a teenager myself as we giggled and tried on clothes together.

But last night, there was an even bigger milestone! Katy and I had our first argument. You may not think that's so good, but it's just as important a step in our relationship as the shopping trip.

It means we feel comfortable with each other, comfortable enough to clear the air and have done with it and come out of it friends.

Nowadays, it's hard to imagine life without Katy. We're all very glad she's become part of our happy family. ■

Summer's Essence

HIGH summer ... Where rose-petals fall
Upon an old, grey, weathered wall,
Two butterflies, tortoiseshell, and white,
Bask in the sunshine's golden light.
Frail wings outspread, so still they lie,
Spellbound, beneath the blaze of sky.

Meanwhile, their gentle brethren go
Fluttering softly, to and fro
Among the multi-coloured flowers,
Pansies, and pinks, and foxglove towers,
Till, drawn by honey-rich perfume,
They seek the buddleia's purple bloom.

But here, upon the old grey wall,
Where satiny-red the petals fall,
Both cabbage-white, and tortoiseshell
Drowse, in the warmth they love so well.
As delicate as lace they seem,
As they sun themselves, and dream.

Oh, the life-span of a butterfly
May seem so brief, to you and I,
Yet Peacock, Beauty of Camberwell,
Swallowtail, Skipper ... who can tell ...?
May yet enjoy, in nature's wild, sweet way,
All summer's essence — in one perfect day!
— Kathleen O'Farrell.

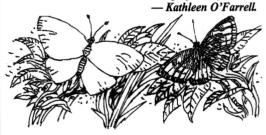

by Lee Cummings

HOME WHERE THE HEART IS

THE enormous snowball flashed and sparkled in the sunshine of the bright December day. Rebecca grunted with effort as she put her shoulder to it. The ball was as big across as she was tall and it took all her strength to roll it into the exact centre of the garden.

Panting with exertion, she surveyed the results of her efforts with satisfaction. It was perfect; the biggest snowball in the world. And it would soon become part of the biggest snow*man* in the world. And she would be his friend.

The sound of distant shouting came faintly from the house.

Rebecca frowned. Climbing on to the giant ball, she sat with her legs dangling, shaded her eyes against the glare and looked around.

Among the distant, snowclad hills a tiny black dot was moving.

She watched it for a moment or two. It was too far away for even her sharp eyes to make it out properly, but it was certainly moving in her direction.

Rebecca became aware that her bottom was getting cold, even through her snowsuit. The suit was meant to be a Christmas present, but Mummy had decided that, because the snow had come, she could open that one parcel a day early and wear it as a special treat.

Rebecca thought it was really to get her out of the house so that Mummy and Daddy could have a fight.

From somewhere in the house came the sound of breaking glass. Rubbing her bottom to restore circulation, Rebecca set off to start work on an even bigger snowball.

Inside the old, stone-built farmhouse, Maddy McSherry stood glumly by the kitchen sink. The view was spectacular, looking out on some of the most beautiful peaks of Scotland's west coast.

In the distance, the slopes of the mountain glittered beneath a carpet of virgin snow. Closer to hand the hills descended, row upon row, to the lower-lying fields where the wild, untamed reaches of the "out-by" gave way to carefully-husbanded "in-by" land.

All in all it was magnificent, but Maddy's eyes saw none of it as she gazed blindly out of the window.

In the living-room Mike McSherry sat, seething unhappily, by the fire. The old, wing-backed chair creaked as he shifted his weight. Nothing he did these days seemed to satisfy Maddy, and yet it had all begun so well. What had gone wrong?

They had bought the farm for the sole reason of escaping the rat-race of urban life. With Mike's redundancy money and an inheritance from Maddy's grandmother, they had suddenly seen a way out.

They both agreed it would be better for Rebecca, too. She could play safely in the countryside, there was a village school just three miles away and, although the farm would never make them rich, they would be comfortably off. It seemed idyllic.

Twelve months later, here the two of them were, fighting like cat and dog.

Rebecca was quite happy, and had settled down quickly at her new school. It only had thirty pupils; there had been that many in just one class at her old school.

Mike was happy, too, although he worked long days, up to twelve hours sometimes. He was always tired in the evenings, content just to watch TV or read.

But he was working with his hands, which he loved, and doing it for the good of his family, whom he adored. He slept well and each morning he awoke to a new challenge. Life for Mike had never felt better.

But Maddy had never settled. No sooner had the furniture been arranged than she had begun to miss her old neighbours, trips to the cinema, even the traffic noise in the street outside . . .

She kept the radio on all day and the television in the evenings. She had the hens to keep her busy, and two cats to keep her company. But she still fretted for human contact, the ability to pop down to the corner shop when she liked, all the small things of town living.

Lately Mike had begun to look on work as a welcome means of getting away from the house. Each morning he would pull on his gumboots and stride rapidly away across the fields, out of range of his wife's nagging.

That evening, after a hard day's work mending fences, something he wished that he could do with Maddy, he had been sitting on a stool in the kitchen removing his muddy boots when she'd begun her usual litany.

The phone was off, the post hadn't arrived, the pipes were frozen, the mobile shop hadn't called . . .

Mike could hardly believe his ears. What did she expect at this time of year? It was winter!

Finally he had snapped.

"If it's so awful, why don't you just pack up and go?" he'd growled, and regretted it instantly.

Mike stared into the fire miserably. In the grate the peat glowed, sending a sweet scent wafting around the room.

He and Maddy had cut and dried the peat themselves. The peat bank came with the farm; free fuel for the rest of their lives. And no heating bills either, as it burned so well in the Aga, providing hot water and heat for the rest of the house, and cooking their meals. Why couldn't Maddy see all the advantages of their new way of life?

Mike glanced out of the big picture window. Rebecca was busy rolling another enormous snowball across the garden. His grim expression softened as he watched her.

R EBECCA collapsed exhausted, face-down across the latest contender for the title "World's Biggest Snowball". Snow was really quite interesting close up, she thought, her nose only inches from the dazzling white surface. Soon she clambered back on to her feet, and she scanned the distant hillsides.

The dot she had seen earlier was now much closer and was clearly a man. It would be some time yet, she thought, before he reached the farm.

She put her shoulder to the giant snowball and set off, gasping and puffing, across the frozen grass to the centre of the garden, where the World's Biggest Snowman would stand.

* * * *

Maddy dusted, wiped and polished until the kitchen gleamed from floor to ceiling. Finally, running out of surfaces to burnish, she sat down on a stool to get her breath back.

She would have to go back into the living-room and face him, of course. The awful thing was that she realised that it was all her fault. Lately it seemed she just couldn't help herself. The days in the house were so long and silent while Mike was away fencing and fixing, and Rebecca was at school.

She slid off the stool and did what she always did in time of stress — she put the kettle on.

Mike was still sitting by the fire when she came into the room, bringing mugs of coffee and a plate of biscuits.

He was working on a plan of the farm, marking the places where work still had to be done on the boundary fence. As Maddy entered, he glanced up uncertainly.

Maddy risked a half smile as she laid the tray on the coffee table next to the plan.

"I'm sorry, Mike," she said stiffly.

He was glad she'd made the first move, but somehow he still couldn't bridge the gap.

"I am, too. Shouldn't have said all that. Sorry."

They each took a coffee and perched, a little way apart, on the window seat, gazing out. And though they both looked at the same scene, what they each saw was different.

Mike saw Rebecca playing in the snow, happy in the beautiful, untouched countryside. It made the perfect picture.

Maddy saw their daughter running innocently through a garden beyond which rose the hills, cold and menacing.

The snow began to fall again, big, soft flakes, tumbling down like feathers in slow motion. Gradually, silently, it blotted out the hills as Rebecca worked on.

IT was Mike, washing-up the coffee cups in the kitchen, who first heard Speck barking. He made his way unhurriedly through the house to the front porch.

Rebecca, he saw, had been joined in the garden by a tall figure in a long dark coat, and the collie was bouncing round them. Visitors were rare at any time of the year; in this kind of weather a stranger could only mean an accident on the hills or, at the very least, a car run off the road.

Mike hurried out. The snow was coming down in great, swirling flurries.

"Daddy, this is Josh, he lives in the snow and he's come to help me build the biggest snowman in the world!" Rebecca excitedly strung the words together so that she ran out of wind, ending with a great gasp.

Their visitor smiled as he played with the ends of the long, red scarf tied loosely around his neck.

"Mike McSherry." Mike held out his hand, which was quickly grasped and firmly shaken. The eyes looking steadily into his own were very dark, almost black. The face he saw was dark also, tanned. The man's smile broadened.

"I'm Josh Herdman. I'm a landscape painter, but I don't actually live in the snow. I'm renting a caravan on the other side of the hill for a while. My bottled gas has run out, so I've nothing to cook and no heating. I had no option but to pull out, and your house looked nearest on the map. . ."

"Well, you got here just in time," Mike said, looking at the sky. "The light's going."

Josh Herdman looked rueful.

"Yes, I know, it was foolish to set out so late, but on my map your farm didn't look to be so far away."

Mike laughed.

"It isn't far as the crow flies, but when the crow has to climb one hill after another, and in weather like this . . .

"Come along in and let's get something warm inside you." He turned to Rebecca. "You, too, young lady. It will be dark soon; your snowman won't walk away during the night."

Rebecca was too tired to resist.

Over bowls of Maddy's hot soup, it was agreed that Josh would stay until the weather abated, when Mike could take him around to his

A Christmas Welcome

*C*hristmas carols sung by children,
With enthusiastic voice,
Spreading far the Yuletide message,
Helping every heart rejoice.

As the family parties gather
Round the hearth to reunite,
Where the season's reminiscing
Kindles memories to delight.

Now, the church bells ring to welcome
Folk at home and those away,
Linking thoughts of celebrations
On this new and festive day!
— *Elizabeth Gozney.*

caravan. He was welcome to the spare cylinders of propane from the barn.

But the snow continued to fall all that evening, with no sign of letting up.

Although Josh tried to protest he would be more than comfortable on the couch, Maddy would have none of it. She soon had a bed made up in a snug attic bedroom.

The evening passed agreeably, the four of them watching Christmas children's programmes until Rebecca's bed-time. Before she went, Josh had to promise to help with her snowman in the morning.

The outlook for Christmas Day was bright with scattered snow showers, said the weatherman as Mike produced his home-brew and they pulled their chairs in to the fire.

The warm conversation flowed easily over the weather, farming, painting, wildlife. Slowly, it moved on to subjects more closely related to their personal lives. Their likes and dislikes, their common needs, their different ambitions . . .

Maddy found herself telling Josh all the things she couldn't bring herself to say directly to her husband. Yet Mike was there, sitting just across the fire from her so, in a way, she was really speaking to him. It just seemed easier talking to a stranger.

Mike discovered he was listening with a more finely-tuned ear to his wife as she explained how the days on her own had grown longer and longer, how she missed the sound of human voices, the warmth of human contact . . .

Josh listened more than he spoke. He smiled as Mike talked about the long days in the fresh air, the joy of using his hands again, working for himself and the satisfaction of supporting his family.

And Maddy felt ashamed. She knew she was being selfish . . . but . . . Mike cleared his throat.

"Maddy? Once the snow's gone, would you like us to go into town? Not just once — maybe once a week. I'll organise around that. Is that OK?"

"Oh, yes, Mike. Please." Her eyes shone. "And maybe — I mean, I've kept out of the way when you've been working, because I know how busy you are — but if I could come up and sometimes see what you're doing —?"

Husband and wife looked at one another with shy smiles. Maybe something could be worked out.

Then Josh talked about his own life: married at 19, divorced at 21, married again at 30, widowed a year later . . . unable to settle, looking for something and not really knowing what. And always the loneliness.

"It's not so much that she died, but that I didn't love her enough while she was alive."

Maddy shivered, hearing the bleakness in his voice.

He stood up to go to bed, and looked down at them. "I think what I've been looking for this long while is just what you have here. As they say, 'You don't know what you've got till it's gone'. Don't throw it all away, will you?"

And he went upstairs.

"Christmas Day tomorrow." Maddy stretched. "Rebecca will be up at the crack of dawn looking for her presents. We'd better get some sleep while we can."

Upstairs, the bedroom seemed cosier than usual, and quite naturally they turned to each other as they hadn't seemed able to do for weeks . . .

IN the morning everyone was up early. The animals must be fed, no matter what. The snow had stopped, and the day was bright and clear.

Maddy cooked a huge Highland breakfast and they all tucked in with a will. In the living-room afterwards, Rebecca was soon almost hidden in a pile of wrapping-paper. There was a sledge from her father, a half-size violin from Maddy, and smaller gifts from doting grandparents, other relatives and school-friends.

Rebecca squealed with excitement and dashed outside, dragging the sledge behind her.

Mike left to inspect the animals and see to their feeding.

Josh and Rebecca worked together that morning to make the snowman, piling the great snowballs one on top of the other for the body, and making a smaller one for his head.

When he was done, he was very large, and Rebecca proudly thrust a broom into his outstretched arm as she declared him "The Very

Biggest Snowman in the Whole Wide World!"

Josh stepped forward and wound his red scarf around the snowman's neck. It was, he said, his present to her, but only when the snowman did not need it.

"When you wear it you must think of me." He smiled.

Once Mike got back from the fields, they loaded the gas cylinders into the back of the Land-Rover. Despite Rebecca's pleas, Josh wouldn't stay for Christmas dinner, so Maddy provided a box of "Christmas goodies" — a leg of turkey, a huge wedge of Christmas cake and a small bottle of brandy, "to chase the cold away."

Finally they were away, with Rebecca running alongside until they reached the main road.

MADDY busied herself in the kitchen. As she trimmed brussels sprouts and peeled potatoes, she could look out and see Rebecca talking to the snowman and straightening his scarf.

In her mind's eye she saw the three of them, the night before, sitting together, their faces animated in the fireglow. She could hear Josh's words as he told them of his sad, disrupted life.

"You don't know what you've got till it's gone . . ."

She caught herself humming a carol as she basted the turkey, and smiled to herself. It was going to be a good Christmas after all.

Mike returned, stamping his feet in the hallway. The roads were passable, he said, but only just. He'd used four-wheel drive all the way.

He gave her a big hug, which went on until she fended him off with the basting spoon.

The day passed too quickly after that and, by the time Rebecca went reluctantly to bed, both of them were worn out. As Maddy dropped off into a deep, untroubled sleep, Mike thought he heard her murmur, "You don't know what you've got . . ."

All the following week the weather remained cold, with clear blue skies and starry nights.

Mike and Maddy had their hands full, what with routine tasks and Rebecca.

There were no arguments, but Mike wondered how it would be after their daughter had returned to school. He hoped for the best.

New Year's Day dawned bright and sparkling, and Maddy went singing through the house to the front door.

"Dumpty, dumpty, dumpty, dum, when the snow lay on the ground, deep and thick and . . ."

As she opened the door, her voice tailed away. Standing on the doorstep were two gas cylinders and a flat parcel with a note attached.

Mike joined her on the doorstep as she began to read the note aloud.

"Dear Mike, Maddy and Rebecca, please accept this gift as a thank you, not just for the gas but for letting me into your lives for a while.

Christmas always has been the hardest time for me, but this Christmas you made it good. In return I would like to make the new year good for you.

"Sitting by your fire, I could see that you have something wonderful together. You have youth, strength and, with Rebecca, a glorious future.

"It's all in the picture, if you look!

"Happy Hogmanay — Josh."

Together they unwrapped the package, cutting the string and folding back the stiff, brown paper until the picture was exposed to view. There was a long moment of silence as they looked at it.

They recognised the hills and valleys of the familiar landscape at once, with the mountain rising in the distance.

Seen from high up, the farmland stretched away to the rocky coast. In the centre of the scene, dwarfed by their surroundings, stood three figures with their arms about each other.

"Three small figures in a very big landscape," Mike said. "Is that how he sees us?"

"Isn't that how we see ourselves?" Maddy said slowly. "Isn't that what we are? Wherever we go, whatever we do, isn't that what we all are?"

Mike turned the picture to see it more clearly.

"Do you know they are laughing at something, those three?"

"And why wouldn't they be?" She grinned. "There's a lot to laugh at."

Together they walked out into the great white expanse of the garden. The snow stretched crisp and untrodden, in every direction. A hush hung over the fields like a held breath.

A shaft of sunlight stroked the flank of the hill, and suddenly Maddy saw the mountain — really saw it for the first time. How beautiful it is, she thought. And just listen to the silence!

The two of them turned and looked at each other for a long moment. Mike was the first to break the silence.

"And where shall we hang our family portrait?" he asked.

Maddy turned to look across the snowy garden.

"I thought maybe in the hall, so that we can see it as we go in and out. It will remind us of what we have, so that we don't lose it." She looked up at him, and her eyes were sparkling.

"Three small figures in a landscape, but darling, what a landscape it is!"

The kiss they gave each other was more than a kiss — it was a promise.

Then the silence was broken by laughter as Rebecca came running, the snow exploding at her heels, the red scarf flying like a banner at her neck. Coming up to them, she threw her small arms wide and drew the three of them together.

And there they were, laughing, loving; three figures in a landscape. ■

SOMETHING TO LOOK FORWARD TO

by Kate McCullum

IT was seeing the pear tree that had made the decision for her, Tess knew. As soon as she'd seen the house, back in early April, when the tree's every branch was breaking into showers of white blossom, she had turned to Steven, her eyes shining.

"This is the right one, darling! This is it!"

Steven had laughed, following her gaze. "It's a beautiful tree, Tess, but hadn't we better see the house first?"

"Who cares about details like that?" she had responded, with a laugh at her own impulsiveness.

But inwardly, she felt her pulse quicken. This was right — she knew it was.

Steven had done all the right things as they followed Mrs Stewart, the owner, in and out of the rooms. He had checked that the wiring was new, and the central heating efficient. He had examined storage space, tapped walls politely and counted power points.

Tess had drifted into the little bedroom that looked out to the back. It was still and bare, with boxes stacked tidily in a corner but it had a glorious view of the pear tree, whose branches reached towards the house.

Already, in her imagination, a child ran down the lawn, into the shadowy corner, to climb up those welcoming branches.

Steven, his voice echoing between the bare walls, had come up behind her. She'd leaned back against him.

"Do the cupboards come up to scratch?" she asked teasingly.

"Fortunately for you, they do. It's all in very good condition. Bit smaller than we'd hoped but —"

"But easier to afford." Tess's tone had been eager.

THEY had stood quietly, looking out of the window, until a polite cough behind announced the arrival of Mrs Stewart.

"I see you're looking at the tree," she'd said, smiling. "It's a beauty, isn't it? And the fruit's good, too."

"What variety is. it?" Steven had asked.

"Oh, I wouldn't know. It's been here a long while, you see. It's a cooking pear, not so good for eating."

Tess had sighed and turned away. "It's beautiful. I had one like it at home — when I was little, I mean."

Mrs Stewart had smiled. "You'll feel at home here, then."

She'd stopped suddenly, her face betraying embarrassment. "I'm sorry — I should have said, if you choose to buy it."

Steven had smiled as he replied, "Well, I think you can safely assume we'll be thinking about it."

"Seriously," Tess had added, nudging Steven.

"Very seriously," he'd conceded.

Mrs Stewart's face had relaxed.

"This is a useful little room, too," she'd added. "It was my elder daughter's room — the one I'm moving to live with. A handy room for a child —"

She'd stopped, obviously afraid she'd said the wrong thing once more.

But Tess had laughed and blushed and acknowledged that, yes, there would be a child to fill the little room later that year.

And Mrs Stewart had said that it would be nice to see the old house the centre of a family again.

As she and Steven had gone downstairs with Mrs Stewart, Tess turned her head once more. The pear tree had seemed to shine with welcome as the sun broke through the scurrying white clouds.

IT was hard now to remember those cool spring days. Tess sat, hot and fed-up, in the shade on the patio. She couldn't get much farther these days. She was too round to do any weeding, and the garden looked a mess.

The grass was bleached with the afternoon sun which drained the colour out of everything, and the sky was that still, clear blue of perfect late summer days.

Tess poured herself another glass of fruit juice and shifted position slightly. Then the doorbell rang. She sighed, pulling herself up to make her way through to the front door.

A smiling, familiar face greeted her.

"Mrs Stewart!" Tess exclaimed. "How nice to see you again."

"I'm in the area, visiting some old chums for a couple of days. I couldn't resist dropping by to see how you were getting on — and I brought you a little something for the baby."

Tess opened the door wide. "Oh, how kind! Do come in. It must be strange to have to ring at your own doorbell."

The other woman chuckled. "It is, a little. But to tell you the truth, it feels like years since I left, not months."

"I'm so glad — I mean, glad you've obviously settled in so well." Tess led the way through to the patio. "Can I get you some tea?"

Mrs Stewart wasn't having any of that. In a few moments, she had Tess settled back in her chair while she herself put the kettle on.

"I'll find everything," she assured Tess, and she was soon back with a tray of tea things.

As Tess began to pour, she was aware of Mrs Stewart looking round.

"I'm sorry that you're seeing it like this." Her words tumbled out. "You see, I haven't been able to do much recently and Steven's been working a lot of overtime."

"My dear, it's your house now. And I certainly wouldn't expect you to be out mowing the lawn with only — what is it, a few weeks before the birth?"

Tess nodded. "Five."

Mrs Stewart was exactly the right person to talk to. She was full of reassuring stories of her daughters' children, and Tess found herself relaxing for the first time in weeks.

As the tight lines around her mouth eased up, Mrs Stewart concluded, "You must be looking forward to it now."

Tess managed a smile. "Yes, of course. And Steven too."

She looked down at the little knitted cardigan that Mrs Stewart had brought and stroked it gently.

"You've got a lot on your mind, though." The words were quiet and full of understanding.

Tess's eyes suddenly filled with tears. "Oh, it's so silly! I know it is. Everything's going well and I'm so lucky to be here in this nice garden, but I still don't feel I belong here."

Mrs Stewart patted her shoulder gently and the little touch made Tess warm to her even more.

"Moving is always hard," she said. "It takes time to make new friends — and you haven't family near, have you?"

Tess shook her head. "That's part of the problem, I suppose. I'm lonely.

"But when we came here in April, the house was so warm and welcoming, and the garden was lovely. It was like a dream."

"I know you were taken with the pear tree."

"I felt at home here then. I remember playing in the garden at home myself," Tess explained slowly, "and climbing a tree just like this one."

"And your child will do the same. What's wrong with that?"

Mrs Stewart's eyes followed Tess's to where the tree with its heavy branches, dull green in late summer, were pulled down by the growing fruit.

"Well, I was an only child and so was Steven," Tess went on. "My mother loved me, I know, but she was never the demonstrative type — and my father worked away a lot. They moved to Canada just after Steven and I married."

Tess remembered those days and the photos of herself, a serious-faced little girl with straight, brown hair cut in a thick fringe, and brown eyes staring at the camera with an expression always slightly surprised.

"When we bought this house, I could just imagine a child playing in the shadows there, hiding on the little path by the hedge, and climbing that pear tree. A happy little child surrounded by love. But what if — what if —?"

Tess floundered uncertainly, her eyes seeking reassurance from this woman who had seen her own children playing in the garden.

Mrs Stewart poured another cup of tea and looked thoughtful. "Tess, dear — if you'll allow me to say the sort of thing I'd say to my own daughters —

"You're frightened you won't be a good mother because you were a lonely little girl — is that right?" she went on.

Tess nodded.

"There's nothing wrong with wanting for your children what you missed yourself. Now I wanted education for my three — I left school just after my fourteenth birthday and so did my husband.

Beyond Compare

THROUGH the stately home we strolled, enthralled by all we saw.
Such treasure! Such magnificence! When, through an oaken door
A glorious garden tempted us . . . "Come on," it seemed to say,
"The past has gone — now gaze upon the beauty of today!"

And so, we took a little path, and wandered at our ease,
Now in sunshine, now in shade of ancient, spreading trees,
In utter peace, though overhead we heard the wild doves call,
Till came in sight, to our delight, the fairest spot of all.

Enclosed within a hedge of box, ten thousand roses grew,
Roses, rich and velvety, of every lovely hue,
Deep crimson, coral, apricot, pale yellow tipped with flame,
Varieties both old and new, with many a charming name;
Some peachy pink, all fragrant in the sun,
Some creamy white, some golden bright, but perfect every one!

As butterflies and bees skimmed past, on little fragile wings,
I thought of that great treasure-house, so full of precious things,
So beautiful they were, beyond the power of wealth to buy,
And then I knew, day-dreaming there, beneath that dazzling sky,
No ornament, no work of art, could ever quite compare
With one dew-spangled damask rose, in sparkling summer air!
— Kathleen O'Farrell.

"We wanted them to have more chances than we had, to go to college if they wanted, to travel the world. We all have dreams for our children," the older woman pointed out.

"I want to be such a good mother." Tess laughed shyly.

"Then you will be," Mrs Stewart declared, with another comforting pat. "You'll be able to give your child a lot of love — and that's the most important thing. A happy family has to start somewhere."

"Thank you," Tess said quietly.

They sat for a moment in the still heat of the afternoon, gazing down the garden. Tess wondered what memories Mrs Stewart saw there, memories of her own children's games and the sound of their laughter.

As if reading her mind, Mrs Stewart turned to look at her and said, "I can still see my younger daughter setting out her dolls down there for a tea party!"

Tess chuckled. "I played with dolls, too, but I'm afraid I was a bit of a tomboy."

Mrs Stewart laughed.

"So was I!" she confided, with a smile that went back half a century.

"You've made me feel better," Tess thanked her with sincerity. "It's nice to think of another happy family here before us. That's a good tradition to carry on."

"There's been plenty of laughter scattered around this house over the years," Mrs Stewart agreed.

After a moment, Tess said thoughtfully, "Perhaps I'll write to my mother tonight. I haven't written since we moved in here."

They sat together and chatted through the afternoon. Tess learned all about Mrs Stewart's son and two daughters and their families and the new house, and she related in turn how well Steven's new job was going so they could save money for the coming baby.

When they parted on the doorstep, Tess held the other woman's hand and said, "And you'll come and visit the next time you're here?"

"I'll be glad to."

Mrs Stewart closed the gate behind her with a wave and Tess stood on the doorstep waving back. For the first time, she felt truly settled in her home.

WHEN Steven came home from work that evening, Tess was still sitting on the patio, wrapped up against the early evening chill. She was rocking gently and humming to herself.

An airmail letter to Canada lay sealed and waiting for a stamp on the table nearby. A casserole bubbled gently in the oven, its rich smell filling the lamplit house.

His arms came around her in the familiar way. "You look happy."

She turned her face up for his kiss. "Have I been horrible?"

Steven hugged her close. "Never that, darling."

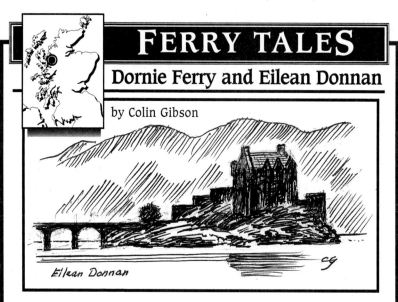

FERRY TALES

Dornie Ferry and Eilean Donnan

by Colin Gibson

Eilean Donnan

It's still called Dornie Ferry, though the ferry over Loch Long was made redundant when a bridge was built to replace it over 50 years ago.

In the same way, Broughty Ferry, near Dundee, still retains its former name although it is over 30 years since the Queen Mother opened the Tay Road Bridge.

Dornie itself is an attractive village in a charming Highland setting. Once over the bridge, you are on your way to Kyle of Lochalsh and Skye. But, in passing Eilean Donnan castle, you will probably pause to take a photograph or two. Or like me, you will reach for your pen and sketchbook to capture its beauty.

The long grass rippled gently and, in the cool evening light, the border didn't look overgrown, but soft and pretty.

"I'm really looking forward to the future now," Tess told him as they sat together and gazed at their garden, hearing the trees rustle like paper. "Mrs Stewart came to visit me today and she told me all about her family growing up here.

"I feel like I belong here now. After all, I may not have much family of my own but —"

"But we're making our own family now," Steven finished for her. "Don't worry, sweetheart. This is a grand old house, and I love you — and everything's going to be fine."

In the last of the light, the ripening pears gleamed golden.

"We're going to get a good harvest this year," Steven said, looking up at the tree with satisfaction.

"And next year, and the one after that, and the one after that," Tess promised, thinking of it all and smiling. ∎

CAROL drummed her fingers on the steering wheel of the car and sighed.

"Oh, please get a move on, can't you?" she muttered under her breath.

Ahead of her, the offending car took the sharp bend steadily and carefully. Carol, who knew every twist and turn of the narrow road and was normally patient with those who didn't, sighed again.

She'd be late to open up the shop at this rate.

Ahead of them, the steep-sided valley opened out and water gleamed, in the distance, shining silver against the dark colours of the surrounding mountains.

Carol knew the car ahead would slow down. Tourists always did, to look at this marvellous view.

She herself gave it only a fleeting, uncharacteristically impatient glance, and then pressed her hand on the horn.

The driver ahead pulled over to the side to let her past.

Carol knew she should wave her thanks, but really! She'd had about enough of tourists, she told herself crossly.

They came here every summer, enthusing about the scenery and then went home — never to be seen all winter when life wasn't quite so easy.

As she passed, she caught a glimpse of a tall young man at the wheel. His car was a large, shiny, red four-wheel drive.

Carol sniffed again. More money than sense, she told herself.

But, against her will, the beauty of the morning made her pause as she made to whizz briskly on. Although she'd never admit it, there'd been a time — not so long ago — when she too would have smiled with pleasure over the sight of "her" loch.

"You never get tired of it,"

A BREATH OF FRESH AIR

she'd tell the tourists who came into the shop for their groceries. "I've lived here all my twenty-two years and I still love it!"

She'd been naive then, she told herself fiercely now.

What good was a hill or a distant view? It was people you needed around when life was dreary, and if they failed you . . .

In the village, the little green-painted frontage of the shop was bright and welcoming. Already, a customer was waiting hopefully outside.

"I'll be open in twenty minutes," Carol told the woman, thinking of the shelves to be stacked and fresh produce to be laid out.

"Oh." The young woman

**by
Kate
Hardstaff**

looked disappointed. "I just wanted some boiled sweets for my son. We're off out for the day and he gets car sick. You know how it is . . ."

Resignedly, Carol stood back to let the woman in, pointedly locking the door behind her. She did try to be hard-hearted but it never worked.

And now, on the doorstep, was Mrs Miller from over the way. She'd set out, still in her slippers, as soon as she'd seen Carol arrive.

"I've run out of eggs, Carol, dear, and Jim does like a nice soft-boiled for his breakfast."

"You need to be tougher, love," her father had always told her, in the days when he'd run the shop and she had been his assistant. "They'll come back."

But Carol, soft-hearted as Mrs Miller's eggs, had never been any good at saying no.

Ushering out her neighbour, she stopped suddenly. Outside, a shiny, red four-wheel drive was parked. A tall young man was climbing out of it.

His eyes went immediately to her own battered vehicle. Then he turned to see her in the doorway.

WE'RE not open," she said at once.

A smile lifted one side of his mouth.

"At least now I know why you were in such a hurry," he said.

His tone was polite, but it made Carol flush.

"Some of us do have jobs to do round here," she said defensively. "If I stopped to admire the scenery every time I drove to work, I'd never get here."

"I'm sorry I held you up. I pulled over as soon as I saw it was safe to do so."

Carol, the twisting road with its blind corners fresh in her mind, knew he was right.

She turned back into the shop, feeling embarrassed.

"I'm open in a quarter of an hour."

"I'll wait. I'm in no hurry." Again the faintly amused tone in his voice needled her.

She went back in, banging boxes around with unnecessary determination while she filled her shelves. The milk crate was waiting in the cool yard round the back and she lugged it in without bothering to unpack part of it, as she usually did.

Against her will, she found herself laughing at her own bad temper. Fury was obviously good for the muscles!

The hands of the clock ticked round and outside, a tall figure still lounged in the square.

Carol sat down on an empty box and sighed. Oh, she wasn't used to being this grumpy. And she did love life here — her busy village shop, her little cottage attached to her parents' house a mile or so up the glen.

There, the only sounds were sheep and the wind in the trees.

But it had all soured for her since last summer. This spring's arrival of tourists had only brought it all back.

Jon had arrived last year in a bright, new four-wheel drive he'd hired. He'd been overwhelmed by the area, eager to explore and happy for someone to show him round. Carol had been equally overwhelmed by his laughter and fun, the breath of excitement he'd brought with him. They'd gone climbing together on her days off from the shop.

A student, he'd had the luxury of several weeks' holiday and he seemed to have spent most of it with Carol.

And then autumn had come, and his letters had been infrequent. He'd come up again once, as the leaves were turning, but he wasn't alone that time — he'd brought a friend and the two young men went climbing together that time.

Carol was plainly off the scene.

Then the name Susie had been mentioned and a sharp look had passed between the two friends. Carol had known then exactly where she stood.

A T half-past eight, she reluctantly unlocked the door again. The tall figure was gone.

Carol felt a momentary disappointment.

Then she saw him, across the little square, at the window of the climbing shop. Stewart was putting up a fax of the day's weather forecast. The young man was looking over it with him.

She'd been right — another man exactly like Jon. Here to climb mountains . . . maybe break hearts.

She tossed back her hair and turned back inside.

He came in a few minutes later, smiling as he passed her at the counter.

Carol nodded.

He moved around the shop, picking up some cans of cola and a packet of biscuits. Then he stopped by the postcards.

Carol found herself watching as he selected a view.

A postcard landed on her counter.

"I'll take that one. I'll write my message on the peak."

"How nice." Carol smiled, insincerely. "Is that why you climb them? To write wish you were here?"

Showing off, she thought inwardly. Rushing from one mountain to the next to prove how many you could do, and never stopping for more than a few minutes . . . Just like Jon . . .

"In a way." He grinned. "My grandfather used to walk all these hills; he was the one who got me interested. So now, whenever I go up a hill he told me about, I write him a postcard from the peak, describing the view. I wish he *was* here but at least he gets the card."

Carol looked away from his open face, embarrassment at her uncharitable thoughts making her flush a little. She rang the items up on the till in silence then, in a softer tone, she said, "I hope you have a good day."

"Thanks. I've got the weather for it." He began to gather up the goods. "Do you walk much yourself?"

She glanced out of the window to the outline of the peaks. "Oh yes, I have done."

"Perhaps we could go for a drink later? You could tell me the best routes." His smile was friendly, his gaze direct.

Carol turned away.

"I don't think so, thank you."

"I'm sorry. Am I trespassing?"

He was looking at her ringless left hand.

Carol shook her head.

"Only on my privacy." But the words weren't said as harshly as they sounded and the young man didn't seem offended.

"My grandad loved this area," he said with a grin. "He met his future wife here."

Carol opened her eyes wide but couldn't think of a response. With a cheerful farewell, the young man swung out of the shop, into his car and was off.

Carol tried, between customers, to rouse herself to anger again. Another young man, coming here looking for a bit of romance as part of his holiday before going back to his daily life, she told herself.

She remembered Jon, sitting beside her on the summit, one glorious summer day.

"This view is spectacular, the weather's great — and you're just the icing on the cake, Carol!" he'd said.

She'd laughed at the time, until she realised he'd really meant it. She wasn't an essential part of Jon's holiday — just an added extra.

But she already knew about this man's family and she'd only spoken to him for five minutes!

L OCKING up was at five-thirty. At five-twenty, the bell on the shop door rang sharply and a sturdy, wind-ruffled figure came in, bringing with him a breath of mountain air.

Somehow Carol wasn't surprised.

She turned from the bars of chocolate she was unpacking and couldn't help smiling. The young man's hair was tousled, his face glowing and healthy, his grin wide. He looked tired but thoroughly happy and she held out a bar of chocolate to him.

"You look like you could do with this."

He took it with a word of thanks

"You should have been there. What about that drink and I'll tell you all about it?"

"You don't give up easily." She couldn't help smiling at his eager face.

"Not on something that's worth it."

The words sounded like flattery, but the tone was genuine. Carol gave in, with more pleasure than she'd realised.

"I'll be finished here in half an hour or so."

"Great! I'll nip back for a shower and pick you up at six!"

He turned away, then paused.

"Where's the postbox here?"

"On the way to the pub. Is that the card for your grandad?"

He nodded.

"I'm sure it means a lot to him."

They shared a smile.

"Look, you'll want to park outside the pub so shall I meet you there?" Carol suggested. "I can post it on my way."

He hesitated a long moment and then reached into his pocket.

"All right, thanks."

He put the card down rather deliberately on the counter in front of her. The writing was uppermost and she instinctively looked away. It wasn't polite to read other people's post.

As she locked up, though, she had an idea. She'd just accepted an invitation from a young man whose name she didn't even know. Maybe it would be fun to surprise him when he arrived.

The name would be at the bottom of the card. *"Will"* he'd signed in clear dark handwriting. That was a nice name.

"Hello, Will," she'd greet him casually when he arrived.

Against all her good intentions, her eyes went over the writing on the card and a familiar word jumped out at her.

"Carol."

Carol? How did he know her name?

She skipped quickly over his description of the view from the summit, trying not to read how clear and silent the air was, how he was sitting there in sun looking right out towards the sea.

I may not move on to the next youth hostel, it read. *Maybe history repeats itself. There's a girl called Carol here whom I'd like to know better.*

When Carol set out to stroll along the main street, the postcard was still in her pocket. She was deep in thought, trying to contrast Jon with Will.

She knew she should be suspicious. She knew she shouldn't fall for the same line twice. And yet . . .

There was something about this young man. There was something about his enthusiasm and energy. There was perhaps, Carol realised, something in herself that was tired of winter and the long dark nights spent regretting last summer.

It was well into spring now. After all, last summer had been fun while it lasted. Maybe she shouldn't have expected so much. Jon had never promised he'd be there for ever and she'd never asked more of him until her pride was hurt.

She sat down on a bench outside the little pub to wait in the evening sun, until a car turned into the yard.

She held the card in her hand as he came over, not trying to hide it from him.

He stopped, looked at it then looked at her. He smiled.

She caught a hint of shyness in the smile. There was steadiness in the hazel eyes that met hers.

"Wish you were here?" she said. "I suppose I was meant to read it?"

His eyes danced in return.

"Not when I wrote it. But when you offered to post it . . . I'm afraid I couldn't resist."

"I'm sorry I was rude this morning." Carol stood up, finding herself comfortably reaching to his chin.

"Tourists can be a pain, I'm sure," he said quickly. "Always driving too slowly, raving about the same old scenery, saying the same old things."

"Sometimes it's nice to be reminded of things. And you can say the same old things in new ways."

"And that makes all the difference, does it?"

"Yes," said Carol, with a smile that forgot the past. "All the difference." ■

WHEN Miss Grace Allenby, who never had any mail as a rule, and very rarely a visitor, was invited to a wedding, excitement rippled through St Anne's Home for the Elderly, on the outskirts of Brynchester.

Gilly Richardson, care assistant, who'd been off-duty for the weekend, heard the good news when she reported back to work on Monday morning. She was delighted!

Although her job often needed a great deal of patience, compassion, and often a sense of humour, Gilly found her chosen career very satisfying, and wouldn't have changed it for any other. She had a genuine affection for the old folk in her care — even the awkward ones!

To look at her, with her laughing face and charming confusion of long brown curls, one would have thought Gilly had little in common with octogenarians and upwards, but she firmly refused to

ALL DRESSED UP

By
Kathleen
O'Farrell

143

acknowledge the existence of any age-barrier.

"I'm so pleased for you, Grace," she said, as she began her breakfast duties. "I bet you can hardly wait till Saturday. We'll make you look really stunning. But whose wedding is it?"

"It's Peter's wedding," Grace Allenby answered. "He's my great-nephew, but I forget his other name." Then a lovely smile lit up her rather craggy face. "When he was small he was the dearest little boy ever . . . he had a soft toy called Mrs Piggywinkle, a little pink pig in a dress and bonnet . . . But I've not seen much of him since."

Grace's memory came and went, so that she lived half in the present, half in the past, and was often mixed-up. She was able to walk with the aid of a stick, and Gilly felt she did very well for someone of her age.

At one time, Grace had read a lot, and had enjoyed watching television, but now found it difficult to concentrate so she sat by the window, gazing out at the big chestnut tree, alone with her thoughts.

WHEN she saw Moira from the office, later on that morning, Gilly asked her more about the wedding.

"It must have been an eleventh-hour invitation," she said.

"Oh, it was." Moira nodded. "Grace's great-nephew, young Peter Wilcox, rang up. He's marrying a girl from the other side of Brynchester, and he suddenly remembered his dear old auntie was living here, and wondered if she would like to go. He thought it'd be a treat for her, and Grace seemed keen, so they're sending a taxi for her. We're to have her ready by twelve o'clock."

Grace had some rather nice dresses. The smarter ones were little-worn because she so rarely went anywhere, so Gilly and Moira helped her choose.

They decided on a silky one, in a paisley design, in rich, jewel colours.

"I've always loved this dress," said Grace, stroking its soft folds. "And I've some nice shoes to go with it, and my navy-blue hat will look all right, won't it? I wouldn't want to let young Peter down."

The staff assured her she'd look a picture, and that Peter would be proud of her, and though, in her clearer moments, Grace realised that she had only been invited as an afterthought, she didn't really mind. It was kind of Peter to think of her.

A hairdresser came to St Anne's every Wednesday. She was a pleasant Italian woman, who shampooed and set the ladies' hair, but as she wasn't available on Saturday, Gilly promised to see to Grace on the morning of the wedding.

"You're lucky," she told Grace as she combed in the rollers, "to still have such healthy hair. I hope I look as good as you when I'm your age." Gilly was really pleased with her efforts.

Grace, though she'd never been pretty, being rather bony and angular, looked quite distinguished when she was dressed up.

Gilly had set her hair beautifully, the paisley dress looked perfect on her, and with her navy hat, matching shoes and gloves, and a pearl necklace, she was admired by everyone.

By eleven-thirty Grace was sitting in the small entrance hall with her hands folded demurely on her lap, expectantly waiting. She looked like a little girl on her best behaviour, thought Stan, the handyman, as he came through the door with his tool-box.

"My word, Grace, I wish I was taking you out myself, when I see you in your best bib and tucker!" he cried jovially.

The minutes ticked by. People came and went through the door, and still Grace sat there, quiet and unmoving, her face bright with expectation. Twelve o'clock came, but no taxi.

"I expect it's held up in a traffic jam," said Moira, passing by with a tray of pills to be given out. "Don't worry, Grace. It will come soon."

But one o'clock came, and still no taxi. No phone-call either, no hint of any reason for the delay.

A little of the glow faded from Grace's face, but resolutely she remained there, waiting.

The lunch wagons came along, and Gilly, who was feeling anxious, and also rather cross that Grace had been so badly let-down, suggested Grace should join the others.

"Just in case," she said . . .

So Grace reluctantly left her chair by the door, and went back in to eat shepherd's pie and apple crumble with the rest.

Truth to tell, she felt hungry, and something else besides . . . there was a sinking sensation in the pit of her stomach, which she knew she mustn't give in to, or else she might cry . . .

A SLOW but certain anger was building up in Gilly, as she settled Grace at the dinner table. Even-tempered Gilly was hurt and dismayed on Grace's behalf and frustrated, too, because there was nothing they could do. The wedding party would have moved on from the church, and no-one was certain where the reception was to be held, so it was pointless ordering a taxi now.

It was like disappointing a child, thought Gilly, as she viewed Grace in all her finery, waiting patiently for the taxi. How could young Peter Wilcox be so cruel?

In spite of Gilly's hopes, the taxi still hadn't come at three o'clock, when she went off duty.

"All dressed up and nowhere to go," the words of an old song rang in Grace's head as she continued her vigil by the door.

It was one of the loveliest days imaginable — a perfect day for a wedding, Gilly thought as she drove home.

After she'd showered and changed out of her uniform she put on her prettiest summer dress. Her mother looked up expectantly.

"We've got time to go into town to choose new curtain material for your bedroom."

Gilly, restless and unhappy, shook her head.

"Do you mind if we make it another day, Mum?" she said. "I'm just not in the mood for shopping today."

"I was so pleased that you were on early today! I thought we could choose the material at Berryman's and then . . ."

"Sorry, Mum," Gilly interrupted her mother's flow, "but I think I'll have to go back to St Anne's. Something's cropped up. I won't be in for supper. But I promise to go with you to Berryman's next week."

Gilly didn't want to say too much as she was sure her mother wouldn't understand about Grace and the way Gilly felt about what had happened to her. She gave her mum an apologetic hug and rang the Home, to see if there had been any developments. Moira told her there had.

"Peter, the groom phoned, wondering what had happened to his great-aunt, and when we told him that no taxi had arrived he called back later to tell us the taxi firm had lost the booking to pick up Grace. He realised she'd be disappointed but now the party was over. He said he'd arrange to send a piece of cake, and they'd come round with the photographs to show Aunt Grace, after the honeymoon.

"Would you believe it?" cried Moira, in exasperation. "Grace took it quite well, though. She's just going to get out of her glad rags now."

"Don't let her," urged Gilly, an idea already formed in her head. "I'm coming straight back."

HALF an hour later Gilly's red Mini was dipping through the leafy lanes of Lincolnshire, with two happy people on board. The sun still shone in a sky of dazzling blue, corn stood golden in the fields, and poppies made ribbons of flame along the roadside.

"Oh, this is a treat!" Grace sighed. "What a dear, good girl you are!"

And Gilly Richardson, who was going to spend money she couldn't afford, knew she wouldn't regret one penny of it — not if that's what it took to redress the balance . . .

"We're coming to a nice tea-garden presently," she said. "I've been there before with one of my boyfriends."

Gilly shook her head when Grace asked, in her quaint, old-fashioned way, if she had a "best boy."

"No, I don't want to be serious with anyone yet," Gilly explained. "Not for a few years, anyway, though I have some good pals."

"I had a best boy once," Grace confided. "He was called Harry, but he died of pneumonia. He was only twenty-five." She paused, lost in thought, and then continued . . . "I never met anyone else I could love in the same way. That's why I stayed single."

Special Lady

There's a lady who appears
To wear so well throughout the years
Of joy and laughter, doubts and fears —
Granny.

In the strange age-juggling game,
She knows the rules, but just the same,
Looks oft belie the name —
Granny.

Her trips down memory lane are spent
Recalling times less affluent.
She knows what hard times really meant
— Granny.

In her youth she'd likely swoon
O'er Gary Cooper, or the tune
That Mr Crosby liked to croon —
Granny.

That lady holds an honoured place,
And more so if she proves the case
She's glowing, growing old with grace —
Granny.

— J.M. Robertson.

She went on, talking of days gone by, and Gilly realised there was a lot more to Grace than she'd realised. The quiet, elderly lady had once been vibrant and bright like Gilly, with a job she loved and a home filled with laughter and love, just like she had.

The tea-garden, filled with people of all ages, from little, laughing toddlers upwards, was as welcoming as Gilly expected it to be. A friendly waitress found them a table near the dovecote, where they could smell the honeysuckle, and other plants in nearby flower-beds.

"Let's spoil ourselves." Gilly laughed, as she ordered the full afternoon tea. They enjoyed dainty sandwiches, scones with strawberry jam, and delicious plum cake. It all tasted marvellous, sitting there in the sunshine, in their best outfits, in such pleasant surroundings.

They watched a young family come up the path, with a little dog.

"You know, Gilly, memory's a funny thing," said Grace pensively. "I can't remember what we had for lunch today — yet I can still see the puppy I was given on my fifth birthday. The dearest, sweetest little golden Labrador."

The glorious afternoon passed pleasantly in the tea-garden for the two women, and when the shadows lengthened they continued on what Gilly called their mystery ride.

After a few miles they stopped the car again, this time beside a large reservoir to enjoy the sight of the sun going down. It was incredibly peaceful there — just water and woodland all around and the most colourful sunset that either of them had ever seen.

As if to complete the picture, a skein of wild geese crossed the violet sky, on their way back to the fens, and the sun, just about to slip behind the horizon, tipped their splendid wings with gold.

"I don't know about you, Grace, but I'm hungry again." Gilly broke the spell. So, to round off their outing, they had a supper-time snack in a small, white-washed inn before driving home.

And when they arrived back tired, but refreshed, after their day, another surprise awaited them . . .

Moira came out of the office to greet them. She was holding a lovely bouquet of flowers, a bride's bouquet, which she handed to the astonished Grace.

"This came for you, Grace," she said. "It was handed in by the bride herself, with her young husband standing behind her, looking rather shame-faced. They were on their way to the airport and were both very apologetic."

"I should think so, too!" cried Gilly indignantly, but Grace was much more forgiving.

"It wasn't really their fault," she said. "So don't be hard on them, Gilly. They didn't know about the taxi firm losing the booking until it was too late. It doesn't matter a bit now.

"Come to think of it," she said, smiling now, her eyes full of an older, gentler wisdom, "I might have felt a bit out of it anyway, among all those strangers. I couldn't have enjoyed myself half as much as I did with you, Gilly. Oh, that was a treat, your mystery ride — it was all so beautiful!"

Then, as Moira put a kindly arm around her, saying she must be more than ready for her bed, Grace pressed the fragrant pink and white flowers against her cheek.

"They couldn't have had a lovelier day for the wedding, could they?" she murmured happily. ■

I DON'T think I'll ever really understand grown-ups. I mean, Mum cried so much when Peter went away, I thought she must have used her life's supply of tears.

"It's only for six months," he said consolingly.

"But that's for ever! And to India!"

"The world's a small place these days, Mum," my brother pointed out. "And I'll have a whole three weeks with you when I get back."

It made no difference, of course, she still cried buckets. What baffled me was why she did it all again the minute he returned!

I was thrilled to bits and grinning ear to ear, especially when Peter started to unpack.

Mum got a set of ornamental elephants , big, medium, small and teeny-weeny, which she lined up on the mantelpiece and swore to polish every day — and she would. That was another thing I didn't understand.

Still, Peter seemed to. What's more he understood the way I felt as well, because he didn't bring *me* anything to dust!

"Wow!" I breathed as I folded back the crinkly tissue paper.

"You like?" He grinned.

"BAUBLES, BANGLES AND ?"

by Helen McKenzie

"Like? That's the understatement of all time!"

"Twenty-four," he said.

I counted as I put them on and he was right. They were an armful, glittering, narrow, golden bangles making tinkly music every time I moved. I don't suppose that they were real gold, but that didn't matter to me.

"I'm never going to take them off," I vowed. "Not ever."

And I didn't, even though I didn't get much sleep, because with twenty-four of them, whichever way I lay there always happened to be one that dug itself into me.

In the morning when I dressed, I pushed them carefully inside my sleeve and buttoned down the cuff to keep them out of sight. Just wait, I thought, till breaktime and I could show my friends what treasures lay beneath that boring, white school blouse!

K ATHERINE ANDERSON!"
I jumped. I had been miles away, imagining that I was lazing in the shade of some enormous tree and sipping lemonade while, in the distance, elephants were working.

The teacher's voice returned me to the classroom with a nasty jolt. It was Miss Mather's first term at Barnes Street Comprehensive and, as we'd only been back for a month, I hadn't got the measure of her yet. She was extremely pretty, with a turned-up nose, blue eyes and masses of unruly curls, but looks weren't everything.

Some of the wrinkled oldies were as kind as kind could be, with gentle voices. Miss Mather's voice was anything but gentle when she called my name.

"Stand up!"

I shivered slightly and obeyed, praying that she was simply trying to assert herself as boss.

"Katherine Anderson, you know the rules?"

"Which rules, Miss?" I mumbled, trying to avoid her gaze and, in doing so, discovering there was a flash of gold distinctly visible around my wrist. *Those* rules, I realised!

"No jewellery in school," she said.

Well, there wasn't any point in trying to deny my crime. I'd gone a very hot and guilty scarlet by that stage. There didn't seem to be much point in telling her how Peter'd brought me all this Oriental treasure, either.

Anyway, Miss Mather called me to her desk.

"Confiscated," she said briskly, as she dropped all twenty-four bright bangles in her brief-case.

"I'll return them to your mother after school."

"She doesn't come to meet me, Miss."

"No matter. I'll just walk you home myself."

"She won't be there, Miss. She'll be — she'll be out," I blurted desperately, knowing what a ticking-off I'd get from Mum if I turned up with Miss Mather. She didn't like me breaking rules at best, but getting her embarrassed, too, would be the last straw.

"She's shopping," I said feebly.

"I'll wait till she gets back," Miss Mather answered firmly. "Shopping doesn't take all day."

PETER happened to be in the garden when we reached the house. Of course, he didn't know Miss Mather or suspect her mission, so he gave us both a friendly smile.

It was a very nice smile, too, because his face was tanned which made his blue eyes bluer and his teeth shine pearly white.

Miss Mather hesitated for a moment, then she asked for Mum.

"She's out," Peter said. "Can I help?"

"I'm Katherine's teacher," Miss Mather explained.

Peter looked a little puzzled, but he must have gathered from my blushes that there wasn't cause for much rejoicing. I guessed he'd been no angel as a schoolboy because he gave me a sympathetic glance.

"I'm her brother," he replied. "Perhaps you'd like to talk to me?"

Miss Mather shrugged and followed him into the house. He settled her into a big armchair and offered tea so charmingly that she was taken off her guard. Her grim expression softened visibly.

"Right," he said, when she'd begun to sip from Mum's best china. "What seems to be the matter?"

"School rules," she answered in a voice, which, though still cool, had definitely lost the icy edge she'd used on me.

"Oh, dear!"

Peter gave me a terrific frown, which was entirely for my benefit and almost set me giggling. At least, I thought, I had him on my side.

He listened seriously to the outline of my sins, and watched gravely as the shining bangles were brought from Miss Mather's brief-case.

"It's all my fault," he murmured humbly. "You see, I've just got back from India."

"Oh!"

Miss Mather sounded slightly startled and a bit impressed.

"The bangles were a present," Peter explained, "and I must admit that I encouraged Katherine to wear them. Six months' separation is too long, and it was just a way of getting close again."

He flashed Miss Mather yet another of those gorgeous smiles and refilled her cup. It rattled slightly in the saucer as she picked it up and I could tell that he was winning her over.

"Of course," she said. "I understand."

"That's very kind. Some people wouldn't."

Peter's voice was soft, and now it was *her* turn to blush.

Dream Kitchen

*H*OW I loved Great-Granny's house
When I was very small.
A little, grey-stone place it was,
With creepers up the wall.

Her kitchen, twice as large as ours,
Was friendlier by far,
With red geraniums on the sill,
And wild flowers in a jar.

A cuckoo clock — my great delight —
And pictures everywhere,
Slow-burning stove, that gave the room
Its cosy, homely air.

Old calendars, depicting babes,
Or little folk at play,
Still lingered . . . they were much too
sweet,
Said Gran, to throw away.

A big, scrubbed table, where Gran made
Her puddings, cakes and pies,
A dresser — what a lovely sight
That was, for childish eyes.

Gold-glinting plates were garlanded
With blooms of every hue,
While those Gran used for everyday
Had bands of harebell-blue.

Old dishes, though the worse for wear,
Were treasured, just the same,
Because they went back donkey's years,
And bore a famous name.

The rag-rug, jewel-bright on the floor,
Was made by Gran herself,
While family photos clustered thick
Upon the mantelshelf.

A rocking chair — that was her one
Indulgence, but I found
That Tabby Tom dozed there all day,
While Great-Gran bustled round!

Oh, how I'd love to travel back
In time, to that dear place,
To see that kitchen, warm and snug,
The rocking chair, the patchwork rug,
And Great-Gran's wise old face!
                    — Kathleen O'Farrell.

"Perhaps this once we could just waive the regulations," Miss Mather suggested. "Provided that it doesn't happen . . ."

"Oh, it won't," I put in fervently.

But she wasn't actually paying much attention to me any more. She was far more interested in my brother.

"You work abroad then?"

"Sometimes. On contracts. I'm an engineer," he told her.

"An engineer? That sounds really fascinating."

There was a pause. I thought that engineering sounded just about as dull as you could get. Another thing I don't understand. I would have bet you anything that my petite and arty teacher wasn't bothered about heavy industry, yet here she was, proclaiming just the opposite! And things got worse!

"I wonder," she said hesitantly, "if you'd come and give our class a talk about your travels. We're doing India in geography."

We were actually doing paddy fields in China, but my protest froze upon my lips as Miss Mather cast a warning glance my way. I swallowed hard and smiled.

"Delighted," Peter murmured. "Perhaps you'd come to tea tomorrow and we could discuss the plan."

"But Mrs Anderson . . .?"

"I'm sure our mother will be only too pleased to meet you."

"She'll be shopping," I said, underneath my breath.

Grown-ups are terrible for trailing out for boring stuff like food each day. At least, Mum is.

"You needn't have," I muttered when Miss Mather had gone. "Invited her again, I mean. You'd got me out of trouble, so you didn't have to lay on all this extra friendship thing."

Peter eyed me thoughtfully.

"I wanted to," he said.

FUNNILY, Miss Mather didn't come straight home with me next day. Instead, she turned up half an hour later and she wasn't in the plain old blouse and skirt she wore to school, but in a smartly tailored dress. I noticed she was wearing lipstick, too, and that her fluttery lashes were much longer and much darker than they usually were.

She added green eyeshadow in the evening when my brother took her out to dinner at an Indian restaurant to finalise his talk — of course.

That's something that I've grasped about grown-ups. They take for ever talking business and they do it best in restaurants, especially the sort that serves expensive food by candlelight and charges the earth for a simple drink.

Anyway, Peter and Miss Mather went out almost every night that week to get the finer details of his talk exactly right. You would have thought that Peter's speech was to be delivered to the Queen and Parliament, not Form 1F at Barnes Street Comprehensive!

Still, it did go very well, I must admit. I know I'm biased, but the other kids in class were full of it for days.

It went so well, in fact, that Peter and Miss Mather spent the last two weeks of his short holiday on yet more dining out to celebrate. Mum didn't seem to mind him being out so much, although, while he was away, she had been going on about how much she missed us having evenings together.

"It's good to see him having fun," she answered when I challenged her. "And Angela is really very sweet."

It wasn't all that easy for me to agree. Sweet's not a word that often springs to mind when you're discussing teachers, though Miss Mather *was* a whole lot softer on us suddenly, and even managed some humour now and then, which must have been directly due to Peter's influence. It wasn't all that easy for me, either, trying to call her Angela at home and Miss at school, but everyone insisted.

Peter's holiday slipped by and Mum was starting to get fussed about his clothes and packing and the like. She spent long hours at the ironing board, while Dad retired behind his paper, sucking softly at his pipe. That's how they were one evening as I happened to be passing through the hall and overheard.

"She's very good for him," Mum said.

Dad gave a sort of grunt.

"A stabilising influence," Mum added slowly. "I hate this travelling of Peter's. If he could only settle down. I'd dearly love to see him more. And Angela might do the trick."

But thanks to Angela, my brother'd spent far more time out of the house than in. His evenings were entirely hers, and most of his days, when she was unavailable, were spent on planning what they'd do as soon as school was over.

"See?" Mum said triumphantly next morning over breakfast. "Told you, didn't I? Peter's re-negotiated, so he's only going for three months this time."

"It's good, although I doubt if Angela had anything to do with that," Dad muttered, reaching for the paper.

He hadn't happened to be standing by an open bedroom window when they hugged each other on the porch the last few nights. He didn't know about the tears and promises of letter writing . . .

YOU'D think they would have all been laughing fit to burst with happiness, when Peter, on his next return, announced he'd got himself seconded permanently to the firm's headquarters barely twenty miles from home. True, there were a lot of smiles at first, but then he started to distribute presents . . .

I thought Mum and Angela got saris until Peter pointed out that Angela's was actually just a length of sheer white silk for making up into a dress and Mum's a piece of blue to cut a suit. All *that* produced was floods of tears!

They should have been in my shoes, if they'd wanted something to cry over — or my sandals, rather. That's what Peter had brought me, very pretty gold and leather thonging, but not quite the same as having all those yards of floaty fabric . . .

He said I was a tomboy and he'd only ever seen me wearing jeans outside school hours so he was going to buy me denims. For walking up the aisle?

It took me quite a session wrestling him on the sofa till he finally came clean. *My* purple silk was hidden in his other bag.

That's his idea of a joke, you see.

I reckon I still don't understand grown-ups, or grown-ups me. ■

ALL *for*

C OME on, you two. You'll miss the bus." Pat Fairfax helped Johnnie shrug his small shoulders into the school blazer and pushed a pair of muddy football boots inside an already overcrowded satchel. Then she gave Sally's hair a quick brush, checked that her PE kit was in the bag and hustled the two children towards the door.

Thursday was always hectic. It was the morning when Pat helped out a neighbour by taking her youngsters to the school bus which left before eight a.m.

It was raining hard, so there was a further delay whilst they zipped up anoraks and tied the hood drawstrings under their chins. They were running late!

Mr Gosling, cheerful as ever, was waiting for them outside the village hall, the engine of the school bus ticking over.

"Morning, Mrs Fairfax. Grand day."

That was what she liked about Mr Gosling. He had an optimistic turn of phrase to meet every kind of weather. A blizzard would be, "Nice blanket of snow, Mrs Fairfax. The children will be enjoying themselves, come play time." A torrential downpour was greeted with, "Just what we need

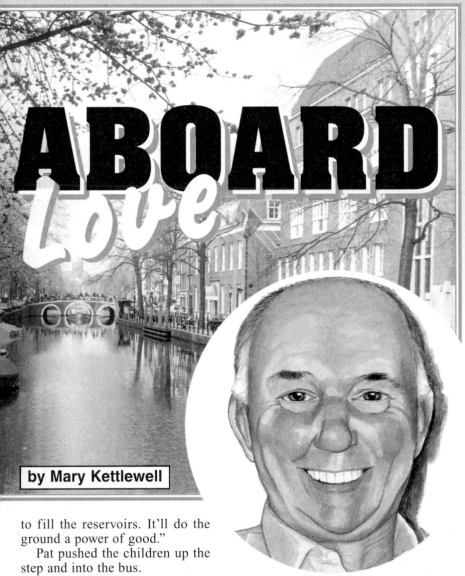

ABOARD
Love

by Mary Kettlewell

to fill the reservoirs. It'll do the ground a power of good."

Pat pushed the children up the step and into the bus.

"Sorry to keep you waiting, Mr Gosling. We had a bit of a problem finding Johnnie's football boots."

"Don't you worry, Mrs Fairfax. Plenty of time."

Mr Gosling knew all his children by name as well as most of the village people. Everybody used him and his bus for their outings. True it was a bit shabby, but his reliability, unfailing humour and reasonable prices made him enormously popular.

He revved the engine, checked

his mirrors and eased away from the kerb.

"Be seeing you on Thursday no doubt, Mrs Fairfax? For the bowls club tour?"

"I've booked a seat," Pat replied. "Let's hope the weather brightens by then."

"Bring your sun-glasses and tanning lotion." He beamed. "It'll be a sizzler. You'll see."

It was, too. By eight-thirty, the sun was already shining and the men were stripping off their pullovers. She found herself sitting in the front row of seats, just opposite Mr Gosling. Her neighbour was deeply engrossed in a discussion with the secretary in the seat behind, over the correct way to mow bowling-greens, so she was able to sit back and enjoy the scenery.

The journey was sprinkled with a cheerful commentary from Mr Gosling. "That's the River Dove we're crossing, Mrs Fairfax. Wonderful stretch of trout fishing. Caught a beauty there last summer. All of two feet long." His square-jawed face broke into a smile. "Give or take an inch or two for fisherman's talk." He negotiated a narrow patch of roadworks, slipping past a gigantic earth-mover with inches to spare.

"I'd be terrified, Mr Gosling. Driving a great bus like this through that gap."

"It's all my practice with the road-trains," he said. "Handle one of those for a few weeks and it makes this little job look like a Dinky toy."

"Road-trains?" Pat was out of her depth.

"What they use in the outback, down under. Two or three wagons hitched together. Eighty yards long was one outfit I drove to Alice Springs."

Pat looked at him with fresh interest. She had always assumed that his life had been spent driving school buses with the occasional outings to Blackpool and Scarborough plus an annual jaunt to the Scottish Highlands in summer.

Come to think of it, he did seem quite capable of driving road-trains across the outback. Hunched over the wheel, he reminded her of a smiling bear. She was quite sure that his muscular, hairy arms, weather-beaten face and imperturbable nature would be a fearsome challenge to the flies and ferocious heat of Central Australia.

"That must have been an adventure."

He accelerated past a row of caravans. "It certainly was. I could tell you some stories you'd scarcely believe." And he did, keeping Pat amused and interested all day.

On the second day of the outing, she arrived early and dropped her coat on to the front seat again. Mr Gosling's embroidered tales of the outback had fascinated her. She wanted more!

But this time it was his turn to ask.

"What of yourself, Mrs Fairfax? Have you ever been down under?"

She shook her head. "Nothing so adventurous. I was house-mistress at a girls' boarding school."

"That must have been some job. All those teenagers!" he chuckled.

"It had its moments," she said. "We took a party of fourth years to France one year. Talk about going grey! French lads followed us around like a cloud of mosquitoes. Love letters, packets of Gauloise being smoked on the romantic banks of the Seine. One girl trying to elope with a Frenchman called Gaspar, old enough to be her father. We had it all."

He roared with laughter.

"And did you get them all back in one piece?"

"Apart from two broken hearts, one lass the worse for wear on the ferry and twenty packets of confiscated cigarettes which we threw overboard — yes!"

"And now you've retired and settled down, the two of you. Husband with a nice bit of vegetable patch and you doing the herbaceous beds."

"Only one of us now, Mr Gosling," she said. "My husband died four years ago."

He looked awkward.

"I'm sorry, Mrs Fairfax. Seems like I've put my foot in it."

"Don't worry." She smiled. "You couldn't possibly have known."

The journey was nearing its end and the bus was entering the outskirts of town. Pat couldn't believe how quickly the time had gone and how much she'd enjoyed the trip.

"Will you be coming on the Mystery Tour next Saturday?" Mr Gosling asked as Pat picked up her coat. "There's still room." He picked up a clip-board. "Nobody's taken that front seat yet."

She lifted her eyebrows and gave him a long look.

"Is that an invitation, Mr Gosling?"

The ex-road-train driver flushed.

"But of a rough and ready way of putting it, I'm afraid."

"Thank you," she said. "I'd love that. Where are we going?"

"You'll have to wait and see." He gave her a wink. "Can't give away all my secrets. Tell you what, though. 'Jim' would sound a deal better than 'Mr Gosling'."

"And 'Pat' would sound a lot less school-marmish than 'Mrs Fairfax'," she responded, touching his arm.

P AT was desperately disappointed when she tripped on the path and sprained her ankle on the Thursday afternoon before the Mystery Tour. She'd been looking forward to it all week. She dialled Gosling's Coaches and left a message on the answering machine.

She waited up until ten o'clock hoping for a phone call from Jim, but the line remained dead and she went to bed feeling thoroughly

by
John
Taylor

The Farmer And His Wife

I'D heard Anne was a dab hand at making a raspberry sandwich cake before I even knew her name. Anne's just corrected me — she says they are Victoria sponges.

How did I know she was an expert at making these mouthwatering cakes?

I had been persuaded by a well-known bantam breeder to enter one of my birds at Cupar Show, and it won a Highly Commended ticket.

Cycling back that evening to our farm, I met Anne pushing her cycle up the hill just past Pitscottie. I got off mine and joined her, and as we chatted I learned she had won first prize with her sponge cake. That's how I knew she was an expert before I even knew her name!

After we were married and Anne invited anyone to tea, a sponge cake was a must.

WE sat the other evening chatting about how nice it would be to cut into one of Anne's sponges filled with home-made lemon curd instead of jam.

You see, for health reasons I haven't had anything that contains sugar for three years now.

Anne suddenly burst out laughing.

"John, do you remember when you made me a sponge?"

I did — only too well!

One Thursday morning it was obvious that Anne was ill.

I rang the doctor and he was at the Riggin before midday.

He said Anne had a bug of some kind and hadn't to get up till he came back again.

"When will that be, Doctor?"

"Sunday morning."

After he had departed, I went up to Anne.

miserable and completely out of sorts.

She was woken at half-past-seven by a peal on the front doorbell. Jim was on the doorstep.

"I only got your message this morning, Pat. What's the trouble?"

She pointed to her bandaged ankle.

"I can't put any weight on it."

"Hang on a minute," he said, running back to the coach. He returned with a folded wheelchair. "This should do the trick."

"John," she began, ignoring her health problems, "I'm having the Misses McNivens to tea on Sunday and I've no sponge cake."

I wanted to go into Crail and let the two dear old souls know that as Anne was ill we'd have to postpone the arrangement. No, Anne insisted she would be up by Sunday, but not having a sandwich cake to offer them was really bothering her.

"Darling, I'll make one for you," I offered, little realising what I was letting myself in for.

I'd never baked anything before, and to start on a sandwich cake was rather rushing in where angels fear to tread, but having promised, I couldn't very well back out.

"Get the scales, John," Anne said, "and put two eggs on one end and weigh equal amounts of butter, flour and sugar. Then I'll tell you what to do."

I went downstairs to carry out her instructions.

Scales and eggs were no bother, and our butter was in pound packs, as at that time Anne made our own.

How much butter was equal to two eggs? I cut a lump and dropped it on to the scales. They shot up and one egg landed on the flagstone floor. Our dog enjoyed that egg.

TO cut a long story short, with several trips upstairs to Anne for further instruction, I reached the stage of beating the eggs and butter together.

What a task! My arm fair ached with beating. Eventually I took my yellow mixture up to Anne's bedside for approval.

I think seeing me in such a state of exhaustion over such a simple thing really amused her.

"Take it down and spread it in your tins," she instructed.

"Which tins?"

"Oh, John, you should have had your tins ready greased. Leave the basin with me while you grease the round fluted tins. You must never stop beating!"

I never knew Anne had so many tins, but at last I found the fluted ones and rubbed them with butter. I suppose that was what Anne meant.

Upstairs again, Anne spread the mixture in the tins, and I was instructed to put them on the top shelf in the oven.

Anne said the timing was crucial — I had to take the tins out of the oven at five past nine.

I went across to the byre, and when I looked at the clock it showed a quarter past nine!

I opened the door with care. The cakes had risen and turned a beautiful brown.

I shouted the state of affairs upstairs to Anne and was told to take them out of the oven.

I must have had the top shelf too near the top, or one sponge had risen too much, because when I pulled it out I left a bit on the top of the oven. It rather spoiled the look of my effort!

Give Anne her due, she said they both looked beautiful and she could easily hide the damage.

THE doctor gave Anne permission to get up on Sunday. She had ample time to make another sandwich for her visitors, but didn't.

I noticed at tea-time, when one of the guests complimented her on the cake, that she was very pleased and hastened to tell them I had made it.

Thank goodness the guests weren't farmers' wives or I would never have heard the end of it at Cupar market!

"But I'm not ready," she protested, pulling her housecoat tighter.

He glanced at his watch.

"Give you ten minutes," he said. "They'll have to wait."

Somehow, he had managed to settle her comfortably in the front seat and they had driven for two hours. The tour had taken them to Scarborough and the rest of the passengers had got off for a shopping break and a breath of sea air.

Jim frowned at the fume-filled coach park with its milling crowds.

161

"I know a nice little spot," he said. "Up on the moors."

He parked on the top of Ravenshead cliffs, facing out to sea, and they picnicked on sandwiches and tea from Jim's flask. The view was breath-taking. Through the open door they could hear the crying of gulls, and they spent several hours chatting and regaling each other with stories and anecdotes of incidents they'd experienced during their working lives. All too soon it was time to pick up the other passengers.

Pat arrived home with her ankle aching fit to burst but feeling happier than she had for months. It seemed as if she had known Jim for half a lifetime.

That next Thursday, Jim was five minutes late with the school bus.

"Puncture! Must have picked up a nail somewhere along the line." He shouted out the invitation just as the doors were closing. "I've got something to show you, Pat. Down at the yard. Can you make it round about five?"

"I'll be there," she shouted.

The Whist Drive could wait. Half an hour with Jim was a far more intriguing prospect, and besides the walk would do her good. Dr Jamieson had told her to start exercising the ankle . . .

She discovered him in the yard, grinning at his new toy.

"What do you think of her?" he said proudly.

It was indeed an impressive sight. Painted in pale blue and cream, the coach had a specially designed front seat for the courier and all mod. cons. The words "Specialist in Continental Travel" painted along the side added an air of glamour.

"Well, you're a dark horse, Jim. When did you hatch this idea?"

"I've been saving for a while, Pat, and all that talk of the outback whetted my appetite for travel again."

"It's magnificent, Jim. When are you planning your first trip?"

"That depends," he said slowly. He wiped a cloth over the coach's already immaculate windscreen. "What's your Dutch like?"

OLDMILLS, ELGIN

*F*OR a step back in time, a visit to this beautifully preserved watermill is a must.

The building stands on the site of Kingsmills, granted a charter in 1230 by Alexander II, and was reckoned to be the first and oldest mill on the River Lossie. Renovation of Oldmills started in 1978 and was completed in 1984. The work included digging out the lades and rebuilding their banks, landscaping the surrounding area, cleaning and refurbishing the building and renovating the mill machinery. A pleasant lade-side nature trail adds to the tranquillity of this delightful spot.

OLD MILLS, ELGIN : J CAMPBELL KERR

She looked startled. "Do I speak it, you mean?" Pat looked at him quizzically.

For once he looked serious.

"I've got a suggestion, Pat. The other driver is taking over the school runs and I'm going to have a crack at driving tours to the Dutch bulb fields. I wondered if you would like to be the courier? Talk through the microphone as we travel. Tell the tourists about Dutch cheese and . . . er . . . that painter, Van Gogh . . . and tulips. You know the sort of thing."

"It's a grand idea, Jim. But what I know about Holland would fit on to the end of an egg-spoon."

"Which is why I've got you this," he said handing her a copy of *The Complete Guide to Holland and The Low Countries.*

"Jumping to conclusions aren't you, Jim?" She tried to give him her "school-marm" look, but it broke into a warm smile.

"Come on, Pat. Taking tourists to Holland will be a rest-cure after those lasses you had in the South of France."

IN just three short weeks Pat and Jim were cruising in the gleaming coach along a road lined with brilliantly coloured tulip fields.

Pat tested the microphone and began her carefully-rehearsed speech.

"Ladies and gentlemen, our next stop will be Edam, the town made famous by its tasty, world-renowned cheese, with the familiar red skin. The town itself has some fascinating mediaeval buildings. In particular, don't miss the ancient Church of . . ."

They reached the market square and the passengers set off, leaving Pat and Jim alone.

"I've been doing a bit of thinking, Pat," Jim started. "We make a good team the two of us. How about making things a bit more business-like in a permanent sort of way . . . ?"

"Just what are you trying to say, Jim?"

He leaned forward and opened a cupboard near the driving seat. The enormous bunch of tulips which he thrust into her arms nearly smothered her.

"Tying the knot. That's what I'm on about, Pat."

She was so touched that she gave him a fierce cuddle.

"So that's how road-train drivers propose is it, Jim? Flowers and tying knots!"

She couldn't take it all in. It was too sudden, and before she'd had time to reply the coach was filling up again.

"Give me a little time, Jim," she said, as he caught her eye, before turning his attention to the passengers climbing aboard.

It was late afternoon and Pat had just finished her talk on the delights of Amsterdam in spring-time and replaced the microphone on its hook to the left of the steering-wheel. She was quite proud of her achievement — so proud that she forgot to click the small black button

on the microphone to the OFF position.

Later, when Jim bent over to whisper fond words in her ear, a husky, passion-filled voice echoed from one end of the coach to the other.

"Pat. Will you marry me?"

It took at least five minutes for the clapping and cheering to die down, and another five minutes for Pat's blushes to subside.

When the passengers had settled down, she checked and rechecked the black button. Then she bent over to the driver. "After that, I've got no choice! I'll have to say, yes."

He put out his arm and gave her hand a squeeze.

"Good for you, Pat, love." He grinned. "I always thought that school-mistresses were sensible women!" He swung the wheel of the bus so enthusiastically round the corner of the Rijksmuseum that he nearly clipped a market stall heaped high with Dutch tomatoes.

She gave him a playful slap on the knee.

"Just you concentrate on what you're doing and stop blowing your own trumpet, young man. Or I just might be changing my mind."

Judging by the warmth in her eyes and the smile that spoke of love, there wasn't much likelihood of that! ■

CAMERON didn't want to waken from his dream. He was standing on a raised platform and people were throwing flowers, cheering and shouting for him.

It would have been nigh on perfect if one insistent voice hadn't said, "Here's your baby, Mr Jones. Wakey, wakey."

Cameron opened his eyes to find six-month-old Rebecca being laid on the pillow beside him and his wife smiling down at him.

"Rise and shine, sleepy-head."

"I was dreaming I'd become head of ICI."

"That's a good omen!" Elaine laughed, glancing at the watch pinned to her navy-blue nurse's uniform. "I'm running late.

"Tilly is watching breakfast television but she's ready for playgroup. Rebecca only needs to be delivered next door."

Cameron gave her a grateful smile. Since being made redundant last year, he usually looked after the house and the children.

Today, because he was due to attend an important job interview, Elaine had taken over his duties to leave him free to concentrate fully on the task ahead.

He reached for her hand and kissed it. "If this job works out you won't have to rush to the surgery any more."

"Won't that be a relief!" Elaine said lightly, but not before he'd seen the little flash of guilt in her eyes.

"I suppose you'll miss your new colleagues when you finish working," Cameron suggested, probing gently.

Her eyes couldn't meet his. "I'll miss my patients more."

He groaned inwardly. He should have known that this would happen. Before she gave up nursing to have the children, Elaine had been Nurse of the Year at the local hospital.

It was little wonder that their GP had snapped her up when she asked about the vacancy at the surgery.

Cameron and Elaine had made an agreement. The minute he found another job, she would stop working and look after the children. Neither of them wanted to employ a childminder.

"You'll feel differently when I'm back at work,"

A TIME FOR SHARING

Cameron said, sitting up in bed and lifting Rebecca high over his head. "The girls prefer having a full-time mum."

"I suppose so," said Elaine, kissing the baby.

"And you can return to nursing when they go to school," he pointed out.

She nodded. "Good luck with your interview, darling. I think you're going to bowl that panel over."

Cameron wished he could share her optimism but smiled bravely as she waved goodbye. He'd been without

by Alexandra Blue

work for five months but had not been without Elaine's support for five minutes.

They were lucky, of course. Elaine's job meant that they could pay the mortgage. They had two beautiful, healthy daughters.

Nothing had altered apart from Cameron losing his company car and there not being the same money for life's luxuries.

Funny, he'd always thought of himself as a modern thinker. He was the first to agree that women should be considered equal in every way.

But after months of cooking and cleaning, struggling to the supermarket with the children, fighting against the clock to deliver Tilly to playgroup on time, he was tired of being a house-husband. He dreaded the thought of failing at this interview.

I WON'T fail," Cameron told his reflection in the dressing-table mirror after he'd showered and dressed.

His suit made him feel good; his dark hair, slightly peppered with grey, felt clean and fresh. He was going to take his wife's advice when he entered that interview room and bowl the panel over.

They wouldn't be able to resist his enthusiasm. He was the right man for the right job. He couldn't wait to get started.

Miss Jackson, the retired schoolteacher next door, had agreed to look after Rebecca.

"I'll collect Tilly from playgroup after my interview," he said, handing her the baby. "We should be home for lunch."

The old lady smiled. "Good luck, Cameron. What's for you, won't go by you."

"Pardon?"

She chuckled at his bemused expression. "It's an old saying which means if something in life is meant for you, then it'll happen. If it's not . . ."

She shrugged.

Cameron didn't want to consider failure.

"And if you don't succeed, it's not the end of the world," she added. "Elaine's delighted to be working again."

Cameron frowned, remembering that guilty look in her eye when he'd suggested she might be able to give up her work.

Thanking Miss Jackson, he took Tilly's hand and set off for the playgroup hall. During the first few weeks of his redundancy, he had been a minor celebrity at playgroup — the only father to play Bobby Bingo at their Christmas party.

Nowadays, his attendance was nothing out of the ordinary.

"Goodness gracious," the playleader said. "You're early, Tilly. Did the alarm clock go off at the wrong time?"

"Don't be cheeky!" Cameron laughed. "I've got a job interview."

"Brilliant! I suppose Elaine will have mixed feelings," the playleader

Softly Eventide

*W*HERE *smooth the waters flow,
And evening brings the
tranquil hour of calm;
Where pastures lush encroach upon
the shore.
Protected by the rising sweep of hills
This place holds its own nostalgic
charm,
And through the trees, the dappled
sunshine spills —
A burst of glory 'ere the shadows
grow.
And dusk begins to dominate and draw
A misty veil across the waning light,
Till darkness folds its mantle o'er the
night ...*

— Elizabeth Gozney.

remarked then, absent-mindedly pleating Tilly's blonde curls. "She loves her job at the surgery."

He didn't need to be reminded of that. Kissing Tilly goodbye, he hurried to catch the bus.

Cameron took a steadying breath when he entered the offices of Goodison and Sons. They were a firm that specialised in computer software, selling and installing their product, educating companies on how to use it.

The job wasn't unlike his last one, though on a slightly lower level of management. Cameron didn't care. He only wanted the opportunity to work again.

The receptionist was too busy to speak to him. She was chatting on the telephone, so Cameron waited by her desk and tried to calm his pounding heart.

"I'll be with you in a moment," she said, disappearing on an errand which was more important than Cameron Jones.

He fidgeted.

Through the open doorway of an office, two of the staff were having a blazing row. Cameron shut his mind to it.

"Sorry about this." The receptionist had returned. "Can I help you?"

"I can't cope any longer. I hate this company!" the office junior cried, staggering into the reception area under a mountain of envelopes.

"I've got an interview with Mr Goodison," Cameron explained.

"Upstairs on the left." The receptionist dismissed him with a wave of the hand, then reached again for the telephone.

TILLY was delighted to see him.
"Carry me home, Daddy," she begged, clasping her little hands around his neck and refusing to let go. "I want tomato soup for lunch."

"With ice-cream on top?"

She kissed his cheek. "Silly Daddy."

Miss Jackson was looking out for them, Rebecca still held firmly in her arms.

"How did it go?" she asked warily.

Cameron pulled a face. "Come and have some lunch with us and I'll tell you all about it."

He liked to think of himself as an expert in the kitchen. He could now stir the soup, feed Rebecca her puréed baby food and hold a conversation, all that the same time.

"The interview went well," he said, as Miss Jackson and Tilly set the table, "but there were so many young applicants I doubt if I'll have got the job."

Miss Jackson tutted her disapproval. "They might surprise you, Cameron."

"I don't think so." He helped Rebecca with her cup of juice. "The problem is, I'm not sure I want the job. When I arrived, they were all fighting and running circles round each other, and it reminded me of how it used to be in the last company where I worked."

"Isn't that normal?"

"Probably! But it made me remember how demanding the computer industry is. A twelve-hour day was normal practice in my last job and I'd hate to go back to that."

His eyes softened when Tilly wiped her sister's dirty face with a cloth. "I'd miss putting the girls to bed, reading Tilly her bedtime story."

Miss Jackson gave him an understanding smile. "When I was a little girl during the Depression, my father couldn't find work so Mother

KILCHURN CASTLE, ARGYLL

THIS ruined stronghold stands on a peninsula near the top of Loch Awe, some four miles west of Dalmally. Occupying the site of a former stronghold of the MacGregors, the present castle dates from 1440 and was built by Sir Colin Campbell of Glenorchy, first Earl of Breadalbane, whose arms with those of his wife are over the gateway.

In 1879, the same gale that went on to blow down the Tay Bridge first demolished one of the castle's tower tops.

KILCHURN, CASTLE, ARGYLL : J CAMPBELL KERR

cleaned in a grand house, took in ironing, and he looked after the children."

"How did he feel about that?" Cameron asked curiously.

"He hated it. He was a proud man and he thought it made him look weak having his wife pay the bills."

Cameron could sympathise. Even after all these months, it still irked him having no proper income.

Miss Jackson sat down with Tilly on her knee. "Funnily enough, we thought he was wonderful. He was a better cook than Mother and had the patience to play with us for hours.

"Then the ironing business took off and they progressed to dry-cleaning. He became managing director of his own company."

Cameron was amazed. "That's a terrific story. Like a fairytale."

"It's all true," she said proudly. "Sometimes you have to swallow your pride — but never lose sight of your potential."

He poured the soup into three bowls and carried them to the table. "I'll think about that, Miss Jackson."

CAMERON thanked Mr Goodison for telephoning, replaced the receiver and did a little jig about the lounge. He couldn't wait to give Elaine the news. She would be cock-a-hoop when he told her.

"Silly Daddy," Tilly said, giving him an old-fashioned look as she dressed her doll in her finery.

"Clever Daddy," he corrected.

They would celebrate. Sirloin steak on special offer from the supermarket and the bottle of red wine left over from their last French holiday should go down well.

Elaine always worked late on a Thursday. By the time she came home the girls were in bed, there was a bath running for her, and Cameron was chopping onions in the kitchen.

"Have you heard from Mr Goodison?" she asked, observing the candlelit table, the wine and the flowers.

"He called this afternoon. Have your bath and then we'll talk."

She nodded, trudging wearily up the stairs while Cameron hummed as he prepared prawn cocktails.

When she returned, flushed and relaxed from her bath, Cameron swept her into his arms and kissed her. "I missed you today. I hate it when you work late."

"It's obviously not going to be a problem for much longer!" She smiled, pointing to the wine and flowers and taking her seat at the table. "I take it you got the job."

Cameron hesitated. How strange. He'd been longing to tell her his news, but now that the opportunity had presented itself, he wasn't sure how to proceed.

"Well, I . . . yes, I was offered it."

"So congratulations are in order ...?"

He noticed her smile was a bit wobbly, which gave him courage. "But I asked them if they'd consider a different set-up."

Elaine blinked. "But I thought —"

"I don't want to be stuck in an office again," he said quickly. "I hope you don't mind."

She stared at him. "Of course I don't mind. So what are you going to do?"

He shook his head, remembering his conversation with Miss Jackson.

"It turned out they've been thinking of letting more employees work from home. They're going to take me on for a trial period. They're even willing provide the extra facilities to tie up with my own computer."

He hesitated.

"The snag is that all this will be on a part-time basis. I can take care of the work they need in four or five hours a day. They're pleased because they will be paying me less. But they've said they won't object to me doing freelance work for other firms. There are lots of possibilities for earning extra money."

"I'm sure there are but —"

"These months at home have taught me the importance of family life, Elaine."

"I'm glad to hear it —"

"I know I've been resenting you going out to work — but not now. I realise how fortunate we are in that you love your job and I'm rather fond of looking after the girls. Why upset the apple-cart?"

She was still staring and Cameron gave a little sigh. He needed to hear her voice, seek the reassurance that she didn't mind him not taking the secure full-time job with the big salary.

"I'm shell-shocked," Elaine said eventually.

Cameron's appetite had deserted him. "But do you mind about the job?"

She grinned, reaching across the table to take his hand. "Not in the least. You know I'd have hated to leave the surgery. I love nursing."

"And I love you," Cameron said, brushing her hand with his lips. Then a thought struck him. "Imagine me doing all those years at university so I could become a house-husband!"

Elaine giggled. "I don't care what you call yourself as long as you have my tea on the table at five o'clock sharp!" ■

Printed and Published in Great Britain by D. C. Thomson & Co., Ltd., Dundee, Glasgow and London. © D. C. Thomson & Co., Ltd., 1998. While every reasonable care will be taken, neither D. C. Thomson & Co., Ltd., nor its agents will accept liability for loss or damage to colour transparencies or any other material submitted to this publication.

ISBN 0-85116-647-4

EAN 9-780851-166476

POBBLES BAY and GREAT TOR, WEST GLAMORGAN : J CAMPBELL KERR